Evans Williams

EA Signals

£7-95

COMING DOWN THE WYE

By the Same Author

IORANA : A Tahitian Journal
THE SEVENTH MAN
A TRUE TALE OF LOVE IN TONGA
COCONUT ISLAND
JOHN GRAHAM, CONVICT
BLUE ANGELS AND WHALES
SWEET THAMES RUN SOFTLY

1943

Capt. J. Evans Williams

E.A. Signals

COMING DOWN THE WYE

by

ROBERT GIBBINGS

With Engravings by the Author

LONDON: J. M. DENT & SONS LTD.

All rights reserved
Made in Great Britain
at The Temple Press Letchworth
for
J. M. Dent & Sons Ltd.
Aldine House Bedford St. London
First published 1942

BOOK
PRODUCTION
WAR ECONOMY
STANDARD

To
DAI REES
of
Llangurig
in the
County of Montgomery

*

ACKNOWLEDGMENTS

So many have helped me in the making of this book that even were I to fill the measure of a page with names there must still be omissions. From E. S., who supplied that provender the ravens failed to bring, to A. M. K., whose pabulum filled many a mental lacuna, with a hundred others in between, I am beholden beyond measure. To the librarian and staff of the National Library of Wales, as also to those of the public library at Hereford, I offer my sincere thanks, and to my colleagues at Reading University I say Hail! even as at this same moment I say Farewell.

R. G.

MAPS

CHAPTER ONE

Plynlimon is the kind of mountain I like. It is neither too high nor too steep, and there are few precipices. In fact, you can't break your neck without an effort. It is a friendly hill.

Once upon a time I travelled to the Pyrenees with E. J. Moeran, in the side-car of his motor bike. He had recently composed his symphonic impression, *In the Mountain Country*, and no doubt crystallizations of this work were appearing constantly before his eyes. My thoughts, however, were of a more mathematical nature. While his vision was carrying him in harmonies from peak to peak, from waterfall to waterfall, and from sunlit mist to vaporous shadow, my whole interest was centred in determining how long it would take a falling body to reach the bottom of a three-thousand-foot abyss, accelerating at the standard rate of thirty-two feet per second per second, in accordance with Sir

Isaac Newton's law of gravitation. Moeran was driving the machine, and I was in the side-car, and invariably the side-car seemed to be on the outer side of the road. There are few protecting walls on those high mountain passes. You just get a clear, uninterrupted view to the very bottom.

There is nothing like that about Plynlimon. It is a place where you can enjoy all the pleasures of height without anticipating any of the inconveniences of sudden descent. Of course there are cliffs, but they are not formidable ones, and he must have a poor head who cannot look down on the dark green waters of the Rheidol Lake and watch the buzzards soaring to and from the overhanging rocks. Only two downward beats of the wings and the great birds sail out into space, wheeling higher and higher in ever-widening circles. Then, uttering their querulous mewing cry, they half close their wings and glide again to their stony perch.

It was mid-winter when I first tried to reach the source of the Wye, on Plynlimon. In the morning, when I left Llangurig, the sun had risen in a clear sky, and was throwing its radiance over the snow-covered hills. To the west the sky was green as olives and the ice-fringed river, reflecting that colour, showed all the lights of an aquamarine. Higher in the hills the water in the tributaries flowed through crystal gorges. It was as if some giant crucibles of molten glass had been spilled along either bank. In sheltered pools, where the water was deep and calm, delicate fern-like plates of ice stretched out to meet each other over mid-stream, but on windier stretches the frozen surface was rippled and polished, and dark as the water flowing beneath. Where there had been a waterfall there were now caverns of ice, festooned with stalactities, the rock faces on either side shining like chandeliers with frozen spray.

Although there wasn't a cloud to be seen small snow-flakes began to fall, each one dazzling bright in the sunlight, and the higher I climbed the larger these flakes became. But they soon lost their brilliance. By midday the horizons were blotted out, and the tussocks of grass at my feet were crested with fresh snow. The ice-flecked stream had become the colour of pewter. The snow fell thicker and thicker, and a cold wind swept down the valley. Soon I became enveloped in this mild blizzard. My only guide was the Wye itself, beside me, now no wider than an old man's jump. Then I found a dead sheep, stretched out stiff and cold under a slab of rock. If that could happen to an animal that's covered all over with a thick fleece what chance would I have, I thought, with no more than a few hairs on my chin. I decided to retrace my steps.

Three months later I was more successful in my attempt to reach the top. The day was diamond clear, with tufts of high white cloud throwing purple shadows over spur and combe, as they sped away to the south. In all directions there was a tumult of hills: on all sides there were glimpses of distant lakes. From the sheltered slope on which I sat I could watch the silver line of the Wye winding towards the old lead mine above Pant Mawr. A mile to the west the Severn started on its course. Behind me the Rheidol had its source in the flanks of the same great hill.

Plynlimon is not a single peak, but a marriage of many, two of its highest points being three miles apart. These and the surrounding country are some of the oldest hills in the world, older by far than the Alps, the Andes, or the Himalayas, yet it is possible almost anywhere on their surface to pick up slabs of shaly rock which show not only the tide ripples of a time when they were submerged beneath the sea, but also the clearly marked tracks of worms who moved and had their being in those seas some five hundred million years ago.

I was at the source of the Wye. After a gentle murmuring underground the water welled up, brushing aside the young spring grass, to form a pool no bigger than a bowler hat. Then gently it glided between rich tussocks of moss and rushes still bent from their load of winter snow, until it tumbled like a shower of sequins over the black velvet of a peat face. The pool below this was wider and deeper, and with every yard of its flow the strength of the rivulet increased. Small streams from successive dells and dingles joined in, and so, between thick felts of sphagnum moss starred with cotton grass, and over rocks long since worn smooth, it frisked and dived towards its first main tributary a thousand feet below.

But a north-east wind in March is a poor help to meditation, and it was not till midsummer that I realized the full glory of the mountains. Then it was ecstasy, ecstasy unbelievable. I was one with the earth, one with the shale and the shingle washed clean by the winter springs. A warm wind swept over the hills, combing the short grasses, caressing everything it touched. I was alone, utterly alone, and for as long as I wished. A gull soaring in the valley was the only moving creature, a sheep bleating from the shadow of a rock the only sound except the wind, the wind in the grasses. Purple and silver the grasses, as they bent in the breeze. And the great mountains heaved and swelled; and the river, a thin silver stream, sprang from gigantic thighs.

It was in these hills, in the summer of 1401, that Owain Glyndwr, of royal blood, cut his way with a small band of retainers through a strong force of the English who had surrounded him in the valley of the Hyddgen. It may have been in these same hills that he ended his life, although Snowdon seems to have been his chief lair, for Holinshed tells us that 'the Welsh rebell Owen Glendouer made an end of his wretched life in this tenth yeare of king Henrie his reigne, being driven now in his latter time (as we find recorded) to such miserie, that in manner despairing of all comfort, he fled into desert places and solitarie caves, where being destitute of all releefe and succour, dreading to shew his face to anie creature, and finallie lacking meat to susteine nature, for meere hunger and lacke of food, miserablie pined awaie and died.' On the other hand authorities to-day seem to think that he died in the house of his daughter at Monnington Court in the Golden Valley (not Monnington-on-Wye, as the guide-books tell us), while the men of Gwent aver that Owain never died but that 'he and his men sit sleeping in Ogof y Ddinas, buckled in their armour, their spears leaning against their shoulders, their swords across their knees. There they are waiting till the day comes for them to sally forth and fight for the land again.'

From Plynlimon, on a clear day, one can see Cader Idris, near whose summit is the Chair of Idris. The man who sleeps a night therein awakes a poet or a madman. But under my feet the turf is soft and warm, and the rippling grass is smooth as a tiger's flanks. There are wide stretches of hill-side where club-mosses, like miniature cypress and fir trees, enrich the texture of the carpet. Though no more than a few inches high they are relatives of the great sixty-foot branchless trees which grew in the tropic climate of these islands millions of years before man appeared upon the earth, and which in their decay formed the seams of coal now so helpful to his existence.

There are stretches, too, of close-growing whinberry on which the caterpillar of the Emperor moth may be found. Big and fat, with a white-spotted, rich green skin, he is as royal in his youth as when, after spending the winter in a silk cocoon, he emerges in the imperial glory of his peacock-eyed wings. You find beetles, too, their heads and tails a lustrous green and their backs shining golden in the sun. In a tussock of moss a few yards from the source a meadow pipit has built her canopied nest of grass and hair, and in it five brown eggs will soon be chipping. On a rock, not far to the west, a family of young wheatears wait impatiently for their parents to return.

Looking up from these I see a range of hills smothered in light. At one moment they might have been swept by a turquoise brush, at the next deep amethyst ravines emphasize the emerald of their slopes. And overhead, clouds, an endless pageantry: towers of foam tossing their heads to meet the frayed threads of moisture that weave themselves into a marbled tracery.

CHAPTER TWO

LLANGURIG IS A LOVELY VILLAGE. If I were Séan O'Casey I'd call it a darling village, and it's not more than ten miles from the source of the Wye. In addition to a church, and chapels of many denominations, there's a police station and a post office. The policeman, when I was there, was a nice quiet sort of a chap, not a bit anxious to cause trouble to any one, though, of course, that may be due to tradition. He had a predecessor who held sway for twelve years, and only brought three men into court in all that time. He didn't like taking people 'up the steps,' he used to say. Instead he carried a strong stick. That kept order better than all the magistrates. And, indeed, it is this man's own son, Dai Rees, who is now the uncrowned king of Llangurig.

From the first moment that I stepped into the 'Black Lion' I felt at home. Quick wits and kind faces. I'm not suggesting that I have either myself, but I like those things. There was Gwilym, who had slept in the Garden of Eden in 1917. He told me that there had only been one tree there, and he couldn't be rightly sure if it was an apple-tree. But he was very wise for all that. There was Ivor Morgan, the bailiff, under whose discretion the river flourishes. There was Old Tom and his friend Old John, who had worked together on the roads for fifty years. It was that same John, the father of pretty Annie, who gave me a blackthorn stick, cut with his own hands from a hedge he'd been laying. Of 'putting down' hedges, as he called it, he told me 'you mustn't twist the branches too much or they won't grow. When you're laying a hedge you're not making a basket. Just enough of a twist to make them spring back and grip the stakes.'

'How long would it last,' I asked, 'after you've put it down?'

'It might be twenty years, but that would be ten years too long,' he said.

Then there was Tom Thomas who kept a bull. It was a pedigree Hereford, and weighed eighteen hundredweight. Tom could let him loose in the yard, and then he had only to go in and hold up his finger and the bull would come and put the ring in his nose on to Tom's finger, and follow him back into the stall. Tom

6

could lie down in front of that bull and it would lick him all over, like a dog. But after four years the bull was getting too heavy for the young herd, and had to be sold. It was a great grief to Tom, and the news that the bull was fretting made him sadder still. The big animal was refusing all food, was refusing to look at the cows that were brought to him, was lowing constantly day and night. It was fretting. So was Tom.

Well, those are the kind of men you'll meet in Llangurig, men who would rather look at their own native hills than at the finest film that ever came out of Hollywood.

I nearly forgot Cobbler. The night I dined with him he told me how he spent his days. 'Rise at six o'clock when there's a chimney in the village to be swept. When there isn't, stay in bed till half-past. Get up then and light the fire, put the kettle on, and have a cup of tea while listening to the seven o'clock news. After news attend to the engine for the village lighting. Then milk the neighbours' cows. Breakfast, and after breakfast a tour of the hills as postman.' In the afternoon there's manure to be spread for a farmer, or seeds to sow, or hay to be cut, and in the evening if there's nothing urgent for cobbling there is someone's hair to be cut.

We had a good day on the hills in a borrowed car, Cobbler, Dai, Jack Rowlands, the mechanic, and myself. Cobbler says it was the best day he ever had in his life, just looking at the scenery. I can't remember a better one myself.

The church at Llangurig is dedicated to St. Curig, also known as St. Cyr, who, by one account, was an unfortunate child that at the age of three had his brains knocked out when defending his mother against the persecutions of the Emperor Diocletian. Giraldus Cambrensis, however, tells of a St. Curig who came into Wales in the seventh century, and whose staff was preserved at the neighbouring church of St. Harmon until the Reformation. On account of its supposed miraculous healing powers it was then burnt as savouring of superstition. According to Giraldus this staff was 'covered on all sides with gold and silver, and resembling in its upper part the form of a cross; its efficacy has been proved in many cases, but particularly in the removal of glandular and strumous swellings; insomuch that all persons afflicted with these complaints, on a devout application to the staff, with the oblation of one penny, are restored to health. But it happened in these our days, that a strumous patient on presenting one halfpenny to the staff, the humour subsided only in the middle; but when the oblation was completed by the other halfpenny, an entire cure was accomplished. Another person, also coming to the staff with the promise of a penny, was cured; but not fulfilling his engagement on the day appointed, he relapsed into his former disorder; in order, however, to obtain pardon for his offence, he tripled the offering by presenting threepence, and thus obtained a complete cure.'

The same chronicler, who, incidentally, was Archdeacon of Brecon in 1172, has other equally surprising tales to tell. For instance, it happened 'that the hand of a boy who was endeavouring to take some young pigeons from a nest, in the church of Saint David of Llanfaes, adhered to the stone on which he leaned, through the miraculous vengeance, perhaps, of that saint, in favour of the birds who had taken refuge in his church; and when the boy, attended by his friends and parents, had for three successive days and nights offered up his prayers and supplications before the holy altar of the church, his hand was, on the third day, liberated by the same divine power which had so miraculously fastened it.' Then there was the unfortunate case at Howden in Yorkshire where 'the concubine of the rector incautiously sat down on the tomb of St. Osana, sister of king Osred, which projected like a wooden seat; on wishing to retire, she could not be removed, until the people came to her assistance; her clothes were rent, her body was laid bare, and severely afflicted with many strokes of discipline, even till the blood flowed; nor did she regain her liberty, until by many tears and sincere repentance she had showed evident signs of compunction.' Equally remarkable, he says that 'it appears from the ancient and authentic records of those parts, that during the time St. Elwitus led the life of a hermit at Llanhamelach, the mare that used to carry his provisions to him was covered by a stag, and produced an animal of wonderful speed, resembling a horse before and a stag behind.'

From such curious events it is not far to mysterious happenings which occur in our own time.

For example, I was told of a hare that could not be shot. Every evening it would come out and sit on a certain rock in the valley, but no one could shoot it. Cartridge after cartridge was let loose at it, but the hare never did more than lollop away unharmed. At last a man in the village—and this is Llangurig, mind you—went to a wise man, or conjuror, as he is called, and this wise man gave him a sixpenny bit and told him to put it into his cartridge instead of the shot. The next time the hare appeared the man took careful aim and fired. The hare let out a squeal and dashed off, trailing a wounded leg. It made for a small thicket, close by a cottage, and there it was lost to view. But the man with the gun, anxious not to be thwarted, went to make inquiries of the owner of the cottage, and looking over the half-door he saw the old woman lying on the floor in pain. She said she hadn't seen any hare, that she had just broken her leg.

This was told to me by a man who firmly believed that it had happened in his own valley within the last few years, yet I heard a similar story in Ireland thirty years ago, and any one who has studied the subject of werewolves and witches will know that in one form or another the tale goes back to the beginning of recorded history.

But the real point is that the conjuror was wise. And there *are* conjurors alive to-day who can work miracles when all the powers of science have failed. Indeed it is whispered that members of university agricultural departments have visited these men on dark nights to seek cures for troubles that have baffled them. And with success.

Llangurig and the surrounding district has long been famous for these wise men who can counteract the power of witchery.

Like other specialists they need a fee which must be paid in silver. One of them, who lived in Llangurig, and died only a few years ago, required thirteen pieces of silver. From the poor these might be threepenny bits, from the 'middling off' they would have

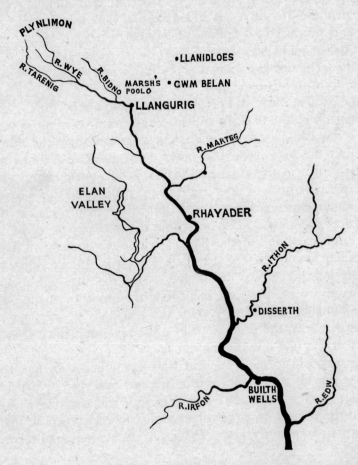

to be sixpences or shillings, while from the wealthy it would be florins or crowns.

There was a case, for instance, of a cow that turned so vicious that none could go near to milk her. The difficulty arose after an old woman had been denied a cup of milk, and it was thought that in consequence she had 'witched' the cow. In his perplexity the owner consulted a wise man, who, coming to the farm, opened a Bible at the last chapter of Ezekiel, which treats of the wiles of the devil, and laid it on the cow's loins. Thereupon the animal became 'as docile as a Christian,' and allowed itself to be milked as meekly as any other in the herd.

Usually the cure prescribed is in the form of a charm which can be hidden near the site of the trouble. They have been found wrapped up in old stockings and hidden in walls, or in bottles among rafters.  These charms, scribbled on fragments of paper, follow a more or less standard pattern, finishing with a medley of hiero- glyphics, suggesting astronomical signs, which are flanked on the one side by a triangular abracadabra, and on the other by a wheel pattern which includes numerals, initial letters, and undecipher- able symbols, said to be akin to the seals used by the popes of the Middle Ages in their bulls. The following is one of the simpler texts:

'Marcus ✳ Lucas ✳ Johannes signum sanctae crucis Dendat this cow or cowes and cafes, amilis, praesentibus, praeteritis and futuris, interioribus and exterioribus. That is the sign of the ✳ cross. Defend this cow or cowes and cafe or cafes and Boll and bullocks and horsces, peges or swine from all evils present, past, and to come, inward and outward. Amen, Amen, Amen.'

This is a more elaborate composition:

'In the name of the Father and of the son and the Holy gost Amen ✳✳✳ and in the name of the Lord Jesus Christ the redeemer and saviour he will relieve Richard Davies and Gwarnas his mare that is bad now from all witchcraft and all evil diseases Amen ✳✳✳ Gasper, vert, myrrham, marcus, melchior, balthasar, aurum, nomine Christi qui regum salvator cum orbe ab auris caduco albo Amen ✳✳✳ Anathemam maranatham dicunt pasitis Sarah adver- sus arti Tabalis Amen ✳✳✳ Eructavit cor meum in noctem in vanum dicam cum atagera subrigi Amen Labia mea pones audas meam anuntiabit veritatem cum tenebra omnia inquiret Lingua malingua subvertatio a Lord Jesus Christ lannen in Labratus the harm and the miseries of Richard Davies and Gwarnas his mare that is bad now from all witchcraft and evil men or women or spirits or wizards or hardness of hart Amen ✳✳✳ and this I will trust in the Lord Jesus Christ my redeemer and saviour from witchcraft Amen ✱✱✱ and this I trust in Jesus Christ my redeemer and saviour he will relieve Richard Davies and Gwarnas his mare that is bad now from all witchcraft by the same answer as would cause the blind to see and the lame to walk and the dum to talk and that thou findest with unclean spirits as writ hath it amen amen amen ✱✱✱ the witch compased them about but the Lord will destroy them all pater pater pater noster noster noster ave ave ave maria audeas factum ✱ an ✱ adony ✱ tetragrammaton amen ✱✱✱ and in the name of the holy Trinity and of their number it preserve all above named from all evil diseases whatsoever Amen ✱.'

Under Llangurig 'parochial news' in the *Advertiser* for 24th January 1894 we read of a custom which has only recently died out:

'The Vicar hopes to abolish the custom of holding the spade for offerings over the remains of the dead at funerals in the parish churchyard.'

This referred to the grave-digger's right to hold his spade over the open grave after the coffin had been lowered and to demand from each of the mourners present a silver coin. In the case of a wealthy family the chief mourner might be expected to put in gold. The vicar's letter called forth a storm of protest and the custom died hard. 'It was the grave-digger's fee and people saw no reason why he should not receive it openly at the funeral and not privately from relations only.'

But let us drop in to the 'Blue Bell.' That man in the corner with the two dogs has trained one of them to answer to Welsh and the other to English. In that way they never mistake orders, and there's no confusion. That old man in the corner is nearly eighty. His wife is dead, and his children married. He lives alone, and gets up at five o'clock in the morning just to hear the birds sing. That chap with the rosy cheeks and the bushy eyebrows, lighting his pipe with the red-hot poker, is talking about the old cobble-stone floors or 'pitched' floors as they are called. His father's house had one till the inspector came and made them take it up and put down concrete instead, as being more sanitary in a dwelling-house. 'Real lovely it was. Oh, a real picture. Throw a bucket of water over it and give it a scrub with a good stiff broom and then a rub with a cloth and it was something beautiful. No harm ever came from a bit of earth, and the pattern was a picture. Real splendid it was to look on, with a circle here and a square there, and another there, and there, and there, and a half circle, in between and maybe a few diamonds. I tell you if a man had a hand to write a story on it he could do it.'

That's Captain Hughes just come in.

Chorus of 'Any fish, Capt.?'

'Not a rise.'

'Wind's too cold,' says one.

'Water's too clear,' says another.

'Gin-clear,' says the captain.

'Time, please,' calls our host.

'Time for one more,' say several voices in unison.

'Drink 'em up quickly,' says the host, as he serves a last round.

CHAPTER THREE

IT WAS NOT MANY MILES from Llangurig, one fine July afternoon, that I met a man whom, for the sake of disguise, we will call Rhys. There are plenty of that name in and out of Wales, and it might be any of them. It is as well, maybe, that I should not describe him more than to say that he was in his middle thirties, that he was wearing a blue shirt, had long wading boots over his trousers, and carried a towel on his arm.

'Coming for a swim?' he asked.

Of course I'd met him before; in fact, we'd been out on one or two private expeditions; to Abbey Cwmhir, for instance, where the headless body of Llewelyn, the last Welsh Prince of Wales, was buried.

'Anything you like,' I replied, for the day was too hot for walking, and I was being devoured by the horse-flies which abound in the valley.

'Seen any fish?' he inquired, as he led the way downstream.

'I saw a couple with dark backs, in amongst those weedy stones at the corner.'

'Ground feeders,' he said. 'Surface feeders are always brighter.'

'Fish can change colour quickly,' I told him. 'I've seen a blue fish change to brown in three seconds in the tropics.'

'Trout can't change their habits,' he replied. 'You look at their heads. The mouth of a surface feeder is cocked upwards: a ground feeder's lower jaw is in a straight line with his belly. I'll tell you another thing, the flesh of the ground feeder is a deeper colour from feeding on shrimp, more like the salmon. I think I'll have a dip in here,' he said suddenly.

'But there isn't a foot of water,' I exclaimed.

'You take the towel,' he said, 'and my shirt,' as he pulled it over his head. Then he waded into the stream, and next moment he was lying flat on his stomach on a little island that with several others stood in the middle of the river. Leaning over the edge he began to explore under the banks with his hands.

'Not much here. Oh, but wait a moment,' he said. His face became serious. He wriggled forward among the rushes, and bent down till his forelock was trailing in the water. For a few moments he said nothing, then, slowly raising himself to his knees, he called: 'Catch!' Next second there was a half-pound trout flapping at my feet.

'Nearly always one there,' he remarked unconcernedly, as he waded to the next island a few yards downstream. The same thing happened there, and now I had two good-sized trout in the haversack hitherto reserved for sketch-books and pencils.

From the islands we proceeded to a pool at a bend of the river where overhanging trees might have deterred a less resolute character. Writhing through the interlacing branches, he peered into the dark eddies among the tangled roots and trailing debris.

'Something here, something here. Come in above that stone.' I rolled up my shorts and waded in.

'Get your hand down there and stop him going out that end. Get both your hands down there.'

In the position that Rhys had assumed, half in, half out of the water, with one leg tucked round the stump of a tree, he might have won first prize as a contortionist. By the time I had obeyed his orders I could have taken second prize in the same class.

'Get your hands further down,' he said. I was already embracing a large boulder which pressed my chin upwards in such a way that if as much as a fly had settled on my back the extra weight would have cracked my neck.

'Can you touch him?' he asked.

I couldn't.

'Can you feel anything?'

I couldn't.

'Get your hands further down.'

I couldn't do that either.

'Stay as you are,' he said. 'Don't move.'

Then as gradually as the sun breaks through dissolving cloud a smile spread over his face. He pulled himself back on to the bank with one hand, holding a pound-and-a-half trout in the other.

'If you don't get your fingers into their gills they 'll slip out of your hands,' he said.

'But why do they wait for it?' I asked.

'You can play with them till they 're silly. They like it. Bring your hand up underneath and tickle them. See if you can get one under that stone,' he added. 'It 's a likely spot.'

I bent over and groped in the shadowed water. Sure enough, and to my surprise, I soon found myself stroking the sides of a fish. It was an uncanny sensation, not unlike a dream in its seeming absurdity. I had one arm in the water and, short of doing a nose-dive into the river, I could not bring the other into play. The fish at my finger tips seemed entirely complacent. I was not so comfortable.

At length I deemed that the crucial moment had arrived. I closed my hand firmly round the middle of the fish, but not firmly enough. It slipped between my fingers and shot upstream.

'Why didn't you get your other hand in front of his head? One hand is no good when their head is free. You can't get your fingers in their gills,' said Rhys.

'But I saw you get one in one hand.'

'I 've been at it for twenty years,' he said.

We wandered on downstream and the weight in my haversack grew. 'How many have we got?' asked Rhys.

'Eight, I think.'

'We must get a few more. That policeman from Birmingham wants to take some back with him.'

We had now reached the stones of which I had spoken, and Rhys was thigh deep in the water. Where I stood it was rather more shallow. I was leaning against a boulder holding a dead fish in my left hand, while, with my right hand, I was preventing the escape of a live one. Rhys was busy tickling.

'I 've got him,' he said; 'a grand fish.' He straightened himself up, holding a big trout in his hand.

It was at that precise moment that I heard the click of a reel. Looking downstream I espied a fisherman with rod and line, not three hundred yards away.

'My God, it's the squire,' said Rhys. 'Tell him you're drawing a picture of me. Go and sit on the bank. Don't let him see your bag.'

The squire had obviously seen something, for he abandoned his fishing and came striding up to meet us. I had just enough time to get to my haversack on the bank, sit down, and assume my most innocent air.

'Had any luck?' he asked jovially, behind me.

I started, as if surprised. 'I'm not fishing,' I said. 'Just making a few drawings.'

'I thought I saw Rhys with you.'

'Yes, I'm drawing him. He is posing for me.'

'Where is he?'

'He's there, in the river.'

'Can't see him. He seems to have disappeared.'

When I looked at the river sure enough Rhys had disappeared, disappeared utterly and completely, leaving no more trace on the landscape than a tree that has been felled leaves against the sky.

The squire sat down beside me.

And there was I with Rhys's shirt and his towel on the grass, not to mention my haversack from which the heads and tails of trout *would* protrude, and my shirt and my shorts soaking wet. I tried to talk of the yellow bushes growing in the gravel in front of us. Were they vetches or broom? He thought they were broom.

'Weren't they once used as a yellow dye?'

He didn't know.

Wasn't it wonderful country? River very low just now. I believed the Coch-y-bonddu was the best killing fly. Was it true that the live beetle was no good, as bait, after lunch?

'Rhys fishes with the minnow,' said the squire. "'Tisn't quite the game, you know.'

'He was only posing for me to-day,' I ventured. Then I remembered that there wasn't as much as a pencil mark in my book. 'Just showing me the hills, the river I mean, the pools, and that kind of thing.'

'Can't think where he has got to now,' said my visitor.

'Can't think myself,' I said, only too truthfully. 'He was there a minute ago. He said something about buying hay. Maybe he's talking to those people at the farm. I was trying to draw that farm all yesterday. Curious how difficult some farms are to draw, isn't it?'

'I am not an artist,' said the squire, eyeing my haversack. I had got the fish hidden, but a few fronds of bracken were still sticking out.

'Have you had a swim?' he asked coolly.

'No,' I replied. Then remembering that the towel was wet: 'I mean yes, just a quick one. Nothing to frighten the fish or anything like that.'

'Can't think where Rhys is,' he said.

'Can't think myself,' I repeated.

'You said you were drawing him?'

'Well, just beginning. Quite a small drawing, you know.' I thought of the servant maid's illegitimate baby in *Midshipman Easy*, and how she tried to excuse herself: 'If you please, ma'am, it was very little one,' but I didn't say anything about that.

The old man got up to go at last, and as he walked upstream I hurried in the opposite direction.

A hundred yards down I found Rhys, on the edge of a corn-field, stretching his naked torso in the sun. 'Damn the man,' he said, 'there was a third fish under that stone.'

CHAPTER FOUR

FOR MANY YEARS it was a source of wonder to me that
there should be bogs on the sides and tops of hills when, as often
as not, there was nothing but rich well-drained loam in the valleys
beneath. Many the time I pondered on this as I left the dry
meadows and clear sparkling streams below me, and climbed to
the haunt of snipe and curlew in the wet soggy blankets that
covered the uplands.

It is, of course, a question of drainage. You don't get bogs on
the top of chalk downs where the water can soak away, but you
do get them where, as on the shale of Plynlimon, the soil is imper-
vious to moisture. Where there is stagnation there will be acidity
of the soil and where that occurs there will be lack of decomposition of plant tissue, for decomposition cannot take place
without bacteria and bacteria cannot live in acid water.[1] This
lack of decay soon produces a congestion of dead stalks and leaves
which, in its turn, increases the boggy conditions. So, layer after
layer of fibrous material accumulates, and this eventually forms
peat.

An interesting development in modern science, originating
some twenty years ago in Scandinavia, has arisen from this absence
of decay. Most of us know bog-oak—trees long embalmed in the

[1] The normal acidity of our own stomachs is a most efficient agent in the destruction
of those innumerable microbes that we swallow daily with our food.

black peat, and saturated with its essence—but few of us are aware that under similar conditions even the pollen grains of trees are as well preserved as the trunks and branches. These can be extracted from the peat, and when examined under the microscope reveal all the characteristics of individual species. From this knowledge it is possible to determine not only what trees were contemporary with the successive layers of bog, but also their prevalence in any one area at the time when those layers were being formed. In addition one can follow the gradual advance northward across Europe after the Ice Age of the great forests of warmth-loving trees like oaks, elms, and limes, as they replaced the pioneering pines and birches of colder epochs. Furthermore, many a prehistoric implement or bone has been found in the bogs, and from the pollen grains encased in the adhering peat we may learn not only their approximate date, but also the climate then enjoyed, or endured, by human life. In a sample that I brought back from Plynlimon, taken at a depth of three feet, students at Reading University had no difficulty in finding pollen grains of pine and birch. From their position in the bog and the history of the mountain it may be inferred that they are the product of trees which existed there soon after the Ice Age.

Most soils are full of bacteria, for the most part inoffensive to human beings. It is these minute organisms which in their struggle for existence resolve plant debris into simple solids, liquids, and gases from which new vegetation forms its tissues. Fungi too. We have only to think how quickly moulds form on anything damp to realize how full the world is of their spores. They also help in the work of recomposition. Humus, that all-important word to the gardener, is merely organic substances in process of dis-integration by these agencies.

But to me those hillside bogs are places where the curlew calls and wild ducks splash, places where the snipe probes its long bill into the soft mud, and where the woodcock hides when the drip of wet branches drives it from the woods. On these uplands, too, one may hear the 'tlui, tlui' of the golden plover, and see them for a moment as they swing in swift flight over the hill-crest. I like the legend which tells how when Jesus was a child he was one day playing with other children, fashioning small birds out of clay. But it was the sabbath day, and an elderly Sadducee, passing

COMING DOWN THE WYE

by, not only rebuked the children, but took the birds and broke them into small pieces, to the great distress of the children. Jesus, seeing the scattered fragments, spread his hands over them, whereupon they came together again and took life. And these birds are the golden plovers whose note is like unto the word glory. Continually do they sing praises to the good Lord who saved them out of the hand of the Sadducee.

There can be few bird calls as varied as that of the curlew. Sometimes it is as soft as the note of a dove, sometimes clear as the tinkle of a bell. The alarm note is sharp and harsh. At times the cry trails into the distance like the yelping of a hurt pup. The tenderest of all is, when gliding in wide circles, the male with bubbling trill calls the female to the nesting ground.

I like, too, the way that an old grey owl sometimes rises and lumbers away, or, maybe, a pheasant, lying out, whirrs from under one's feet. And then on those upland bogs there is often the sweet serenity of the mist; a veil that shuts out all the world and grants a privacy, complete as darkness.

Sometimes, of course, that privacy may be too complete. One morning, after sleeping on the top of Plynlimon, I awoke to find that I could scarcely see my own feet. It had been the night of a full moon, and at bedtime the sky was clear, so clear that I didn't bother to put up a tent. It was still clear at midnight, but when I was awakened by the bark of a fox at about five o'clock in the morning I had much the same sensations as a fly must have when drowning in a bowl of milk. Everything was white. Everything was wet.

As such conditions might have lasted for days there was nothing to do but slither to lower altitudes, praying that I might retain control of my movements on the way. All went well for a couple of hours. I missed a couple of 'drops,' and found myself safely in the valley below. Then the gable end of a shed loomed up before me. At precisely the same moment three dogs also loomed up, prancing, leaping, and barking around me as if they were heraldic lions rampant. One of them had some front teeth missing. On whose skin were they broken? I wondered. I thought of a lorry driver I had met a few nights before at the 'Blue Bell,' who had discoursed to me on Aristotle and the power of mind over matter. He said that he hadn't the slightest fear of the fiercest dog, that he would go up to him and put his hand on his head. I wished that he were in my place.

Then a shepherd appeared, and at a word from him the fury abated.

'Would those dogs of yours bite?' I asked, as gaily as I could.

'Oh, they 'd never hurt a sheep.'

'I wasn't thinking of the sheep,' I said.

But he didn't hear me. 'The big one is a bit rough,' he said; 'might nip a lamb.'

'A thick mist,' I said, hoping to appear at ease.

'Be you the man from the "Glansevern"?' he asked, paying no attention to my remark.

'No, I 'm from the "Blue Bell,"' I told him.

He looked at me inquiringly. They like you to explain yourself in Wales. Introductions are important in remote districts.

I told him my job.

'Yes, it 's a thick mist,' he said. 'Thick as a fleece.'

By noon the sun had broken through. Little green butterflies flipped from grass to grass. Brown turbary pools reflected blue sky.

I have walked barefoot on the coloured sands of Tahiti, on the white beaches of Australia, and on the cedar-scented shores of the Bermudas, but none were ever kindlier to the touch than the rich damp sphagnum moss, crimson, green, and white, or the grey dust of the sheep-trodden peat, high on Plynlimon.

CHAPTER FIVE

THERE ARE PLENTY of lakes in Wales, and most of them seem to have a lady in residence, though not always visible. The most famous of these is Llyn y Fan Fach, meaning 'The Lake by the Little Hill,' in Carmarthenshire. The story goes that once upon a time there was a widow who had but one son. This young man used to graze his mother's cattle on the *van*, or mountain, which is neighbour to the lake. One day while engaged in this occupation he espied, sitting on the unruffled surface of the water, as contented as you please, the most lovely young damsel that mortal eye had ever beheld. That was his description, anyway; but, of course, he hadn't travelled far. 'Her tresses flowed gracefully over her shoulder.' Beyond that we are given no inkling of what she was wearing. I myself was warned by a slightly shocked Welsh lady, before I set out for the Wye, that *of course* I must not expect to see any naked nymphs like the one I described in *Sweet Thames*. So presumably this little girl on the water must have been wearing something. It may have been some pretty design of leaves from, say, the water lobelia which occurs on the bottoms of these Welsh lakes, or it may have been just a simple frock of plaited grasses which she could have gathered from the edge of the pool without ever coming to shore. But either might have been risky for a girl who kept cattle. Do you remember the story told by Captain Wilson of the *Duff*, the first missionary ship to visit the Marquesas, how when the ship arrived at the island they were assailed by numerous damsels who swam out from the shore to meet them, clad only in skirts of green leaves? Although the crew seemed highly appreciative of local fashions when the girls came on board, the missionaries were more conservative. They hastened below deck to find some of the cotton frocks sent out by the ladies of England. Unfortunately, while these good men were in their cabins the ship's goats espied the green leaves—they hadn't seen anything so fresh and succulent for weeks—and forthwith broke from their moorings and attacked the girls, fore and aft. When the missionaries arrived on deck again there was more need than ever for the frocks.

23

But to get back to our own story. Suddenly this lady of the lake beheld the young man who, by now in a speechless sort of way, was standing at the water's edge, holding out a handful of bread and cheese to her. Well, of course, she 'glided' towards him, and of course he tried to get hold of her, and of course she eluded him and dived away back into the water, soaking her hair and whatever she was wearing all over again.

The same thing happened next day, but this time she gave him a smile of encouragement before showing him the soles of her feet above the water. On the third day he was more successful, for the lady came ashore, and, after due palaver, consented to be his bride. As is usual, even to-day, there was bargaining on both sides, but he seemed to do very well out of it, for she brought with her out of the lake a fine dowry of horses and cattle. And so they got married, and lived in prosperity and propriety at a farm about a mile from Myddfai, and had three lovely sons.

But one day, on account of some trifle, such as often upsets a household, though in this case thrice repeated, she left him. Calling her cattle after her, she returned into the lake. Even the poor little black calf that had but recently been slaughtered came to life again and followed his parents into the water.

We don't hear anything of the husband after this sad blow to his fortunes, but, whatever his fate or his fortune, it seems that his three sons acquired the habit of wandering by the lake in search of their mother. And one day she came back to them, at a place still called Llidiad y Meddygon, which means in English 'The Gate of the Physicians.' Addressing herself to her eldest son, by name Rhiwallon, she told him that his special mission in life was to relieve the suffering of mankind. Then she gave him a long list of prescriptions with rules for their use, further admonishing him that, with careful study, he and his family could become the most skilful physicians in the country. After that she met the boys more than once, and pointed out to them the various healing herbs that grew in the district. Soon they attained such fame as never was known before. In order that their knowledge should not be lost they committed it to writing, and this learning has been preserved in print by the Welsh Manuscript Society.

But if all this seems a bit fanciful, and no doubt it has been embellished, though not by me, let me tell you that there are men alive to-day who can show you their genealogy right back to that same lady of the lake, and those men are distinguished, not only as members of the orthodox medical profession, but also for their skill in the use of herbs and 'natural remedies.' One of the same family was a physician to Queen Victoria.

Here are a few cures from the lady's pharmacopoeia which might be applied to current ailments.

'Irritability of mind—to calm. If a man be irritable of mind let him drink of the juice of the celery frequently, as it will relieve him of his irritability, and produce joy.'

'To reduce fatness. Whosoever is fat, let him drink of the juice of the fennel, and it will reduce him.'

'To preserve chastity. If you would always be chaste, eat daily some of the herb called hart's tongue, and you will never assent to the suggestions of impurity.'

There are remedies too for 'reptiles in the stomach' and for 'a worm in the tooth,' but these afflictions are no longer fashionable. On the other hand we read that the smelling of musk, camomile, and red roses, and the drinking of wine in moderation, are good for the brain, but that smelling a white rose and frequent bathing are injurious to the brain.

So much for the lady of Llyn y Fan Fach. There was another girl who was caught near a lake on Snowdon, and she lived happily with her captor till one day when helping to harness a horse she was struck, accidentally, by a piece of iron, after which she was nevermore seen. And there are the maidens of Llyn y Morynion. Their story is that they had been carried away from their village by the men of a neighbouring valley, who were short of wives. Their own folk followed the robbers and, in a bloody battle, slew the lot, whereupon the damsels, feeling thwarted by this turn of fortune, and seeing little hope of further adventure, cast themselves into the lake and were drowned, though it is not very long since an old man affirmed to the local parson that he had often seen them coming out of the lake in the early morning and combing their hair.

Lakes are pleasant places, whether you are watching your mother's cattle or merely on the look-out for the bow-wave of a nixie. Many a day I spent beside pools high in the mountains, and others less high in the valleys. Some of them were fringed with rushes which seemed to grow out of their own reflections, others were edged with horsetails like miniature forests of bamboos, or half hidden by the greater spearwort, whose large yellow flowers shine as if varnished. Some pools were dappled with water lilies, others had their surface unbroken even by a rising trout. In one I watched minnows almost leaping on to the shore to avoid the heavy red-finned chub, and newts wriggling from under stones, and caddis flies rising to the surface for their brief aerial existence. Beside another I found the long track of an otter's tail and the pin marks of a water shrew, I even found the closely studded lines of a pair of hob-nailed boots, but never the print of a small and naked foot. One day I saw a bat swimming. How it got into the lake I don't know, but it moved at good speed to the bank, with its head high out of the water, using its wings as a pair of scoops to force the water backwards.

I had great hopes of better luck when I visited Llyn Gwyn, for that is where Gwyn ap Nudd, the king of the fairies, used to live, and I was told that there is still an exceptionally beautiful maiden inhabiting that water. As I approached I found two sprigs of white heather growing on the same stalk. That seemed a good augury. It was a nice little bit of a lake with a nice little island at one end, where we could have been very happy together, with the wild ducks swimming all around, in and out of the pond weed, and the two herons walking the shore, and curlews crying their love song, and all that sort of thing. For a while I sat up on the old earthworks, which some say were formerly a Roman fort, but which others consider to be the remains of monastic fishponds, for I thought that there she could have a good view of me. When that didn't seem to work I hid among the pine-trees in hope that I might get a peep at her. When that failed too my thoughts turned, like those of many another man disappointed in love, towards the church, and I struggled away over the hills to Llanvihangel-Helygen.

The church at this village is a simple building. East and west there are the straightforward gable ends of a cottage, there is no division to mark a chancel, and, except for the Gothic window behind the communion table, there is nothing ecclesiastical in the structure. The other three windows are small square lights, which show no possibility of being opened. On either side of the aisle are ranged old-fashioned box pews, each with its gate, and midway among them, on the north side, stands the double-decker oak pulpit. All the pews face the pulpit, so those of the congregation whose seats are at the eastern end of the nave must sit with their backs to the altar.

Another church at Disserth a few miles to the south has similar furnishings but, there, there is more evidence of mice than of human beings. I don't blame the parishioners. The ancient pews have straight backs, and are nowhere more than nine inches wide. Even the minister has to sit on a six-inch board, and that without a cushion.

I can well imagine the austerity of the services held there. When I was a boy I used sometimes to accompany my father to a small church in the hills, where he was bound to officiate every Sunday. The congregation usually consisted of one stout old spinster, who owned most of the parish, and a family of about eight children, whose parents owned a small farm. The organist, the sexton, and one other child completed the assembly. The organist was a lean woman with a high aquiline nose through which she sang. Nobody else in the church attempted a note. She was a kindly religious soul, who travelled twelve miles every Sunday in order that the church should not be without music. And there were no motors in those days, part of the journey had to be done on foot, and the rest behind a horse. The sexton was a venerable pensioner, seventy years of age, by name O'Mahony, with a wife five years his senior. One Sunday he confided to my father that his wife was emulating Sarah, the wife of Abraham, for the doctor

* B

had declared that they might shortly expect an heir. Unfortunately the symptoms proved to have arisen from a more prosaic cause. But the two old people had the care of a workhouse child, a small boy of the name of Alfred. Alfred would come into church with his foster-father, and be put to sit in the collecting plate, which was raised above the ordinary seat level by an assembly of hymn books. That gave the child a chance to see what was going on. When it was time for the collection he would be put to stand in the pew, after which he saw no more of the service. As the sexton walked up the aisle with the collecting plate, for he always sat at the back of the church while the congregation occupied the two front seats, he would polish the plate with his elbow or the tail of his coat. He could always count on a shilling from the stout spinster, but the children seldom rose to more than a few coppers between them. Sometimes they did not even manage that, and then the old man would look across to me and shake his head sadly. Once when a stray visitor to the church put in half a crown he looked at the coin for a long while, then bowed deeply to the visitor.

There used to be unorthodox incidents in those out-of-the-way churches in Ireland. One minister that I knew slipped one day as he was stepping up to the lectern, and only saved himself by clutching the brass eagle with both arms. Regaining his balance he turned to his congregation and remarked in a confiding tone: 'I'd have been down but for the blessed old bird.' Then he went on with the lesson.

CHAPTER SIX

THE FIRST TIME that I heard the second symphony of Sibelius was after I had spent a night on Plynlimon. It seemed, as I listened, that I was back again on those hills, and that every emotion I had experienced there was now clarified and accentuated. In the opening chords I could sense the calm of evening, with dusk creeping into the valleys; an ominous, calm, for dark clouds were banking over the distant hills. There was the cry of birds, and wind singing through the heather. Clouds piling overhead were mirrored in a peaty pool.

Rain began to fall. Big drops. Bigger drops. Bubbles on the water. Wind and more wind. A deluge of rain. All sounds drowned by the rumbling of the thunder.

A vivid afterglow. Velvet darkness.

Then in the second movement that marvellous plucking of the strings. Sleep. Sleep. Sleep. Deep heavy sleep, undisturbed by passing squalls or spattering of rain. Sleep.

And after the first glow of dawn wild streaks of light shooting up behind ragged clouds. There is a surge and swell of waking life. It is fantasy, of course, but in those tender passages which follow I perceived a human element. A sprite maybe; laughing, leaping, splashing through the soggy bogs. She calls, and together we race from ridge to ridge, from combe to combe, through sun and shower until we find the lake that is at the head of the stream.

Then the music swells with triumph, and a peace that passes all understanding pervades the hill-side. In the fourth movement the triumph heightens. Harmony upon harmony, and exultant peace of mind. Grandeur piles upon grandeur, crescendo upon crescendo, of joy, and glory, and praise.

The next time I heard this symphony was when I was staying with a doctor in Berkshire. We had been discussing the work, and were hoping to hear it on the wireless. He was putting coal on the fire, before we settled down to listen, when the telephone rang. 'Probably a baby,' he said, taking up the receiver.

He listened to the staccato voice, which sounded across the room. Yes. Yes. Had certain symptoms developed? Yes. Good. Yes—he'd be along in a minute.

'I must fly,' he said to me, and I was left alone just as the announcer's voice came over the ether.

I had hoped and expected to be transported once again to Plynlimon but, far from anything like that happening, the very first notes seemed to convey the whole atmosphere of that room my friend had gone to visit. Whereas the opening chords had once suggested calm now they expressed anxiety. And, instead of those winds that silvered the grasses of the hills, and bent each reed beside the pools, now there was pain, and more pain, and fear, and loneliness. All through that first movement I was conscious only of anguish of body and of mind. And this time the plucked strings, instead of suggesting sleep, were but the epitome of nagging pain, dull, nagging, ceaseless, seemingly endless pain.

And so through agony and weariness and utter lonesomeness until, in those ineffably sweet chords which complete the third movement the voice of the new-born child is heard. Then there is joy beyond the telling, and wails that stir every fibre of the emotions, and, following on the great deep chords of thankfulness, there are paeans of praise, and peace, and rest.

The sound had scarcely died on the air when my friend returned. He had on the same old tweed jacket that he had been wearing an hour before. Except that he looked a little tired his expression told nothing. He went to the fire-place and began to put on some more coal.

'Is all well?' I asked.

'Oh, yes, rather!' he said. 'A lovely boy.'

CHAPTER SEVEN

ABOUT FOUR MILES from its source the Wye joins another child of Plynlimon, the Tarenig. If the course of this rivulet is short it is not without incident. Whereas the Wye, in its upper moorland stretches, glides between rich felts of bog, the Tarenig chooses a more rugged course, cutting its way through rock, swirling between boulders, and dropping over ledges into fairy pools.

From the junction of the two streams the river runs between high sheep-fed hills. The water is sparkling clear, and the slaty stones over which it flows are the colour of carnation leaves. It is a 'fierce' little river, flashing up into flood and subsiding again with all a Celtic show of temper. But, for the most part, like the Celt, its course is gay and not too closely constrained by man-made barriers. If it is here to-day it may be there to-morrow. There is nothing solemn about its course: on the contrary, there is laughter in its waters, and its sudden twists and turns are as sprightly as the people who live beside its banks.

These are the waters where in late autumn the salmon spawn. Then, in the rapids between the pools, one may see the hen fish scraping a furrow in the river bed, and the redder-backed cock fish sidling close to her to pour his milt over the eggs she lays therein. But, in summer, purple plumes of meadow grass shimmer beside the banks. Wild pansies and swaths of blue harebells and yellow bedstraw garland the feet of foxgloves, and immature sandpipers bob their almost featherless tails along the dry shingle.

On either side a climb of a few hundred feet will take you to a paradise of solitude, a paradise where not only in the cool of the evening, but in the glory of noon, you may hear the voice of your Creator. Some people like solitude in order to have freedom to think, others prefer to live among crowds so that they do not need to think. Most conversation and most reading and most entertainment is dope to prevent one thinking. So, for that matter, is a great deal of physical exertion called exercise.

Clouds are not things apart from the sky. They are *of* the sky, ephemeral assemblies of the particles of that water vapour with

31

which the whole atmosphere between us and the void of space is impregnated.

Neither are we creatures apart from nature. We are of the

earth earthy, and far closer to the elements than many of us are aware. Take even the season of birth, of which Dr. Ellsworth Huntington of Yale University has made a comprehensive study. He writes: 'The season at which people are born has far greater

importance than is generally supposed.' The children born in
early spring 'have a low death rate in infancy, and the survivors
live to more than the average age. In addition, the births of
persons who achieve distinction rise to high proportions.' He
goes on to say: 'Man is an animal. Like practically all animals he
has a definite seasonal rhythm of reproduction. This rhythm appears
to be an inheritance from a very ancient time, when relatively few
children survived unless they were born at the best seasons. In
our present sophisticated state children are born at all seasons,
but on an average the ones born at the height of the old seasonal
rhythm have an advantage over those born in its other phases.'

Lest any one born in midsummer should be depressed by these
statements, let me add that Dr. Huntington also says: 'If we were
born at an unfavourable season we can comfort ourselves with the
thought that many great and long-lived people have been born at
that same season. Moreover, heredity, diet, and mode of life, when
taken together, doubtless have far more effect upon health, longev-
ity, and achievement than has season of birth. . . . It may be
better to be born of healthy, long-lived, well-nourished parents
at the worst season in the worst climate rather than of anaemic,
short-lived, poorly nourished parents at the best season in the best
climate.'

I like to feel this rhythm. I like to feel that we are not superior
to other forms of creation, but co-equal with them, each in our own
sphere. We are inclined to flatter ourselves on our intelligence,
assuming superiority because other creatures seem lacking in
powers that we have developed. We seem to forget that they may
have powers of which our imagination has no conception. What
do we know of the sensations experienced through the lateral line
of fish? Not much more than a fish knows of thirst. We can
see that every scale along that line is perforated for a nerve ending,
but we can hardly do more than guess at what information those
nerve-endings convey.

Again, we wonder at the migratory powers of birds, and at the
perfect co-ordination of movement when a flock in fast flight
suddenly wheels or, maybe, scatters. That wonder is aroused
because we have nothing similar in our race experience on which
our imagination can build. They say that imagination is concentrated race experience.

Then, take the horse, an animal whose spirit has for generations been broken to man's will. Yet that animal can find its way home, five hundred and even a thousand miles across strange country. Ask any Australian. Nearer home it is a commonplace that cats and dogs will return from long distances. Not long ago, by way of experiment, a dog was taken, in a closed box, by a circuitous track, to a point some seven miles from its home, and then let loose. It found its way home in a few hours. Some weeks later it was taken by different roads to the same spot and again set free. This time it reached home in a very much shorter time, but *not by the same route*. Instead of following its first course, which resembled the arc of a circle, it took almost a direct line, only going out of its way to avoid villages, woods, and human beings. What did it learn on its first journey?

We are amazed at the powers of aborigines in finding their way through trackless forests. Our lack of this power is equally amazing to them. Of course there are exceptions, and we all know people with good 'bumps of locality.' There was once a European who, in a strange district in black darkness with his eyes blindfolded, was able to indicate the cardinal points of the compass.

In a mere matter of degree, how very much more finely adjusted than ours are the senses of many of the 'lower' animals. Whereas the average human being is unable to taste sugar in a solution that is weaker than one part in two hundred, there are flies that can detect it when there is but one part in forty thousand, and there are butterflies that react to one in three hundred thousand. Bees are highly sensitive to ultra-violet light which, normally, we cannot perceive. A dog is able to hear sounds whose pitch is too high for human ears. A moth has capabilities of scent that baffle our imagination. Fabre described an experience of his with the Great Peacock moth, a relative of the Emperor, whose green caterpillar I found on Plynlimon. On the morning of what he calls 'that memorable evening' a female Great Peacock had emerged from her cocoon on his laboratory table, and he, while her wings were still moist after hatching, had put her under a bell of wire gauze. He tells us that he had no particular purpose in view: he did it as a matter of routine, being always 'attentif à ce qui peut arriver.'

That night, at about nine o'clock, just when the household were going to bed, he heard a commotion in the next room, and a moment later his son, 'petit Paul,' dashed in, half-dressed. 'Come quickly,' he called. 'Come and see the butterflies, they're as big as birds.'

The description was not exaggerated, for the Great Peacock is the largest moth in Europe, and measures six inches between the wing tips. Fabre followed his son to find 'une invasion sans exemple . . . une invasion de papillons géants.' Then he remembered the incident of the morning. Candle in hand, he and his son went downstairs. 'The sight was unforgettable.' The great moths were everywhere, flying around the female in her prison, coming, going, rising to the ceiling and dropping again. With one stroke of a wing the candle was extinguished. The moths beat against Fabre's shoulders, they clung to his clothes, they brushed against his face. 'It was like a maelstrom of bats in a magician's cave.' Each night afterwards for more than a week, in such black darkness that 'one couldn't see a hand before one's face,' ardent lovers found their way into the room. Fabre counted one hundred and fifty of them in eight days, and from his knowledge of the country-side, he was confident that few if any had travelled less than a mile. Yet, at a distance of only one inch we humans are unable to detect the faintest odour from these female moths. Because we are unable to perceive the scent we are inclined to say it must be weak, whereas, as Dr. Eltringham has said, 'it may be and doubtless is extremely strong.' In this connection he rightly asks: 'What strength of colour has a scarlet begonia to a person who is red blind?'

CHAPTER EIGHT

EVERY TIME I HEAR the name of Evans, and that's not seldom in Wales, I think of a story I once heard in Ireland. It was about a woman called Hannah Doolan, who lived in a cottage with a thatched roof and a mud floor, at the top of a lane not far from Inchigeela in County Cork. It was a neat house, and a clean one, so far as she could keep it so, but a leak in the roof and an ever increasing family rendered the task a difficult one.

One day a little wizened-up bit of a man came up the lane and asked Hannah if she could spare him a drink of water. Hannah filled him out a glass of milk.

'Could you tell me,' said he, 'where could I find a few duck eggs, because the hen eggs at the hotel don't suit my stomach?'

'Wait a minute,' said Hannah. 'Mary Kate,' said she to her daughter, 'will you go and ask Patsy Cronin for a few duck eggs for the gentleman. I'll send them down to you, sir, at the hotel. What name will I say?'

'Evans,' said he, 'Evan Evans from Cardiff.'

So that evening five duck eggs arrived at the hotel for Mr. Evans, and a couple of days later there were three more, and within a week another five had been delivered. And then Mr. Evans came to say good-bye.

'How much do I owe you?' said he.

'Yerra, nothing at all,' said Hannah.

'But I must pay you,' he says.

'What's a few duck eggs?' says Hannah.

The long and the short of it was that Mary Kate found a two-shilling piece in each of her hands, in spite of her mother's protestations.

Nothing more was heard of the gentleman until one rainy afternoon, about a year later.

'Good evening, Mrs. Doolan, I suppose you don't remember me?'

'Well now, glory be to God! Come in out of the wet. Mary Kate, go and ask Patsy Cronin for a couple of duck eggs for the gentleman. I hope 'tis keeping well you are, sir. Ah, indeed,

36

not too well meself.   There 's one in the cradle since, and there 's
another coming, and I do be hard put to it at times.   Wouldn't
you take off your wet coat now, and sit down awhile?   Mind that
chair: 'tis a bit broken it is.   These children do be destroying
everything.'

She pulled up a sound chair for him.   'Taedy, bring in a bit of
turf.   Patcheen, will ye give the fire a blow?   Glory be to God,
the weather 's a fright.'

Every other day during the following week a few duck eggs
arrived at the hotel, and then Mr. Evans went back to Cardiff,
and there was nothing more heard of him for another year.   Just
when he might have been expected, who should come up the hill
but the lame tax collector, who was also the local contractor,
limping on his iron stirrup?

'We 're destroyed,' said Hannah to her eldest child.   'The
rent is due this eight months.   Let ye tell him I 'm gone out,' she
said.   'Tell him I 'm gone down to the town with the money to
pay him.   Tell him I 'm gone out this three hours back.'

'Come out of that and listen to me,' said Mr. Jeremiah Mulcahy,
a few minutes later.   ''Tis news I have for you.'

Hannah, under the old feather bed, didn't move.

'Come out from under that bed, Hannah Doolan.   Can't I see
your two feet?'

Hannah emerged.

'How would you like a new house?' said he.

'Oh, to be sure,' said she, 'in the Phoenix Park in the centre of
Dublin, I suppose.'

'Here 's the plans,' said he.

'Plans of what?' said she.

'Your new house,' said he.

Hannah picked up an earthenware jug.   'Now,' said she, 'are
you going before I split your skull with this, tormenting a woman
is seven months gone.'

Mulcahy paid no attention to her.   Instead he unrolled a large
blue architect's plan.   'Here 's a house,' said he, 'commissioned
by Mr. Evan Evans of Cardiff, to be constructed for the benefit and
exclusive possession of Mr. and Mrs. Michael Doolan.'

'And where is he going to build it?' asked Hannah.

'He isn't going to build it.   He 's dead,' said Mulcahy.

'God rest his soul,' said Hannah, crossing herself.

'Overright ye there in the valley it's to be, with yer front door to the sun and five acres of good land behind you,' said Mulcahy.

'Saints of God protect us!'

'He's after leaving the money in his will.'

Hannah looked up at the hole in the roof. 'Well, praise be to God, we didn't mend it,' she said.

It was in a pub near Rhayader that I met ' 'Iggs,' who came from Berkshire, a little old man, neatly dressed, with bright blue eyes in a wrinkled face.

'Very proud to meet you, sir. 'Iggs is my name. I comes from Wantage. Seventy-three, and w'en I goes it's 'ere goes ' Iggs, never did no 'arm to no one, no one never did no 'arm to me. I was in 'Yderabad in 89. Yes, an' 'Ounslow an' 'Ampton Court we did guard, an' didn't we 'ave to sit on our ponies? As still as marble! I 'ad a lovely moustache in those days, could tie it under me chin. But you's an artist. There was a man live near 'ere. Mr. Davis was 'is name. H. W. B. Davis, that was 'im. Do you know 'e painted a picture of that 'ill above Glaslyn, an' w'at d' you think folks in London paid 'im for it? Seven 'undred an' fifty guineas 'e arsks 'em, an' that's w'at they pay 'im. Damn it, they could 'ave bought the 'ole 'ill for fifty quid.'

Higgs chuckled through his long drooping moustache.

'Did you know,' he asked me, 'there's only two straight streets in Oxford, and that's an edicated city? But give me travel for edication. You and me 'as travelled. We're edicated. 'Aven't 'ad a smoke for fourteen days, but this mornin' I says I must 'ave a bit o' 'bacco. Got to 'old pipe in me 'and now, w'en I wants a smoke, but I 'ad a full mouth till five years back; could bend a nail between me teeth. My brother, 'e couldn't put 'is mark on a sausage. Never did lose a tooth till five years back, and never 'ad a 'eadache in me life. Me wife died in nineteen 'undred an' three. Never 'ad no ambitions for another woman. No ambitions,' he repeated meditatively. 'Not that I 'aven't 'ad chances, you know, plenty of chances. But w'at I says is, w'en you falls in love once, real love, mind you, you never does it again, and w'en you breaks your heart once you doesn't do that again neither.'

CHAPTER NINE

IT IS CURIOUS how each tributary of the river and each lake that I visited has become associated in my mind with a different bird. Llyn Rheidol inevitably recalls the buzzards that circled majestically over its bowl, watching for rabbit, field mouse, or small bird off its guard. Those three lakes called Ievan, hidden high in the mountains on the other side of the pass, are inseparable from a flight of duck which, after following the line of a trailing cloud in the evening sky, charged out of the sunset to scoop an iridescent furrow in the water with each pair of upturned feet. I envied them their complete freedom from human cares. No anxiety about shelter, no bother with cooking, no worry about shrinking shirts.

At Leich Pool, near Clifford Castle, there were innumerable coots. For a time, as they swam sedately across the pond, they reminded me of old ladies hunched up in grey shawls, but, needless to say, this image vanished when they turned up their tails, skittish as you please, and disappeared below the surface.

At Llyn Gwyn I watched the portentous strides of two herons. The way they walked one might think their heads were weighed down with a problem in higher mathematics, instead of being just occupied with the idea of finding a frog or an eel. At Llangorse there were thousands of sand martins feeding on the feathery heads of Phragmites, our tallest grass, sometimes called a reed. You can usually tell a grass from a sedge or a rush by the fact that its stem is hollow except at the nodes.

By Caban-Coch reservoir in the Elan valley I saw a willow wren drive away a tree creeper that had invaded its territory, and in the evening I heard the burbling of the nightjar.

So, also, with the streams. Although the meadow pipits are everywhere in the high moorlands, running almost under one's feet in their unceasing bustle for food, it is the wheatear, with its dipping flight from stone to stone and gay flirting of its tail on every resting-place, that remains persistent in my memory of the Tarenig and the upper Wye. Those delicate tints of corn colour and French grey patched together with white make it unlike any other bird that visits us or stays in our country throughout the year. It is more like a dream-bird in a ballet than a reality that shares the same fortunes as the whinchat, stonechat, and redstart.

Edmund Selous also saw this bird as a stage performer, though in rather a different character part. To him the bird recalled a Japanese acrobat who, in throwing a succession of somersaults within his own length, and quicker than the eye could follow, created the illusion of an arch in the air. He was thinking of the birds' pre-nuptial display.

Perhaps I may quote a little of his story: '2.30 p.m. (about). Two male wheatears have for some time been hopping about in each other's company, every now and again one of them making a hostile demonstration against the other. This he does by advancing and lowering the head, with the beak pointed straight forward, ruffling out the feathers, fanning the tail, and making a sudden, swift run towards him. He stops, however, before the point of actual contact, and the two birds hop about, each affecting to think very little about the other.'

This sort of thing goes on until: 'After some time, during which there was nothing specially noteworthy in their behaviour . . . a female wheatear appeared, hopping near them. One of the males at once ran to her, but had instantly to fly before the fierce wrath of the other. The hen then flew to a stunted willow in the neighbourhood, where she sat perched amongst the topmost twigs, the males not following her, but continuing to hop about in each other's vicinity as before.'

After this the display, already described, is repeated again and again by one or the other of the male birds, with the female showing little if any attention. And so the afternoon wears on with but slight variations of the antics. Occasionally the two cocks fly at each other as though to fight, though, quicker than the eye can follow, they avoid an issue. Again and again there is that frenzied dance, like the oriental acrobat. In the later hours they do actually come to grips, but only for brief moments.

Then about a quarter to six o'clock the hen seems to take more than a casual interest in the proceeding and 'it would seem as though she had made her choice, and that this was submitted to by the rejected bird, but just before leaving at six o'clock all three are together again.'

Heighdy! Who hasn't suffered?

The stonechat, with its black head above a white collar, calling 'tchak' from a bracken spray, was the focus of my attention on the Marteg. It had probably wintered in one of the oases of the North African desert, maybe in 'The Garden of Allah' itself at Biskra. A disappointing garden, I thought when I was there, hot and stuffy as a greenhouse. But there would be no shortage of insects for the bird, and it would be a change for it to see the camels passing under the date palms, and the queer black bundles of clothes, encasing human females, going about the streets. There is supposed to be romance in the desert: swarthy men on fiery steeds arrive in a cloud of dust to slake their passion in the street of the Ouled Nails. Maybe they do. I took a walk down that street, and saw nothing that did not fortify my puritan disposition. Apart from that, my chief memory of Biskra is shoe-blacks. As you left your hotel in the morning, with your shoes shining like the negro hall porter's face, an Arab boy was waiting to pester you. Everywhere you went there were these boys with their boxes of boot brushes. If you visited a café there would be one under the table before you could sit down. When you had kicked him away another would arrive and need the same treatment. But the dates in the hotel were good, big dark ones with a thick scale where they joined the stem. Those are the ones to go for. I was told about them by an expert.

The valley of the Marteg was full of children, and their faces and fingers were nearly as dark as those of the Arabs. It wasn't the sun or boot blacking that had stained them, but the juice of the bilberries which they gathered on the steep slopes of the hills. Overhanging the river were elder-trees in flower. 'Flowers of the elder make better wine than the berries,' I was told. 'The best thing in the world for the inflammation—they calls it pneumonia now—we used to call it the inflammation. Drink it as fast as you can; 'tis better than any doctor.'

On the Ithon I watched a dipper walking in and out of fast-running water quite unaffected by the force of the current which submerged it. But when I reached the Lugg I forgot about birds, for in those waters there was once a mermaid. She must have been a serious-minded girl. Although, for obvious reasons, she was not allowed into the local church, she did the next best thing by taking up residence in one of the church bells that, by some mischance, had fallen into the water. She must have been athletic too, for we are told that when the parishioners tried to recover their bell no team of horses could move it so long as she kept holding on to it.

I don't know how it came about that the local conjurer was consulted as to how the bell might be retrieved. The vicar, who presumably was responsible for the bell, should have frowned on such practitioners. Possibly he sent his churchwardens. Anyway, instructions were received that a team of twelve white heifers was to be attached to the bell, with yokes made from the yew-tree and bands from the mountain ash. There was to be absolute silence while the ceremony was in progress.

Success exceeded expectations, for a time. Not only was the bell brought to the surface of the water, but the assembled villagers could see inside it the little mermaid, fast asleep. Whether it was the sight of the mermaid or of the bell which caused the interruption we can only guess, but the fact remains that one of the drovers called out. We are not told what he said. It may have been a word of encouragement to his heifers. 'He called out,' and that woke the poor little girl, who immediately darted back into the river, taking the bell with her. It all happened a long while ago, but folks of Marden have never got their bell back. They say that sometimes it may still be heard ringing in a deep clear pool.

But it is those tree-shaded waters under the bare towering hills above Rhayader which many people consider to be the loveliest stretch of the whole river. There the water rushes, plunges, tumbles, sprawls, and slithers around and over every known shape of rock and stone, rippling, cascading. There are deep shadows under the stones, caverns draped with half-dry weed, when the water is low. There is a sediment on the flatter stones which only a flood will clear away. Singing birds congregate in the choir stalls overhead. A faint breeze stirs the wild pansy, but the poppy capsule does not move and the bramble hangs limp. Families of blue tits chatter as they frisk from tree to tree. A shoal of young wrens is shepherded by an anxious parent. Warblers flit from oak to sally-bush and then back to another oak. A pair of grey wagtails dance from rock to shingle. And the stream goes on, and on, and on.

My friend, Bill Mathers, once wrote: 'Love is birds under trees, over running water.' Most people knew Bill as Edward Powys Mathers, the man who gave us probably the best translation into English of *The Arabian Nights*. Readers of other editions usually skip the verse, knowing how lifeless it can be, but readers of the Mathers translation look forward with eagerness when their eye glimpses poetry on the page.

> 'There's nothing like the blood of grapes
> To give escapes
> From care's infesting, festering apes.
> To set the wit upon probation,
> To give an edge to conversation,
> To make a friend of a relation,
> There's nothing like the blood of grapes.'

That is one of his neatly turned stanzas. Here is another:

> 'The last place where a helper shall be found
> Is in that quarter whence the danger came;
> You would not treat a scalded hand with flame,
> Or give a cup of water to the drowned.'

And again:

> 'When things fall odd,
> Sit down in peace and send your cares to Satan.
> If life's a tangle much too big to straighten
> Give it to God.'

'Bill' was known to a wide public as Torquemada of the *Observer*. Many the time I've seen him in dressing-gown and bedroom slippers padding round his billiard table, turning over the pages of the innumerable reference books which lay thereon.

Among his original works was *Procreant Hymn*, which I published at the Golden Cockerel Press with engravings by Eric Gill. If you can find a copy read it. But be careful. I knew a couple who did so and they had twins within a year.

CHAPTER TEN

IN 1812, a year after his expulsion from Oxford, Shelley eloped with Harriet Westbrook, the sixteen-year-old daughter of a London coffee-house keeper. They were married in Scotland, and, following a short visit to Ireland, came to live in the valley of the Elan, a tributary that joins the main river just below Rhayader. But in 1814 Shelley left her, and in 1816 she drowned herself in the Serpentine in London. Six years later he himself was drowned, in the Mediterranean, and now the house in which they spent some of the happiest days of their lives has also been submerged, and lies far down in one of the giant reservoirs that minister to a city's need.

Much has been written, chiefly in condemnation, of Shelley's behaviour towards Harriet. He himself wrote on this subject to Southey: 'If you were my friend I could tell you a history that would make you open your eyes; but I shall never make the public my familiar confidant.' I think it is probable that only those who have been unhappily married themselves can understand the full import of those words. The others have no right to judge.

Ten thousand million gallons of water now cover the 'wild babbling' rivulet; nevertheless the hills and 'undulating woods' remain, and the cycle of the seasons is undisturbed. In spring each male creature sniffs the breeze, and the bruised grasses lift themselves again, lambs bleat and calves are suckled, children are born and old folk die. In summer the flies pester, warblers glint among sun-freckled leaves, and the valley is drenched with light. Diogenes was once visited by Alexander the Great who asked him: 'What boon do you crave of the all-powerful conqueror of nations?' 'Step aside, Alexander,' answered the old philosopher, 'and do not shut out my sunlight.'

In autumn the crisp leaves whirl like a Bacchantes' revel and pack, one on another, in sheltered waters, as thick and as golden as the feathers on a game-cock's neck. And in winter the sculpturing torrent carves a portrait of its own soul in the rocks below the great Pen-y-gareg dam. Here, for all to see when the water is low, is autographed the fury of unbridled floods, the sweet beguilement of a summer stream.

The water that swirls among these stones is dark and awesome. Close to where a footbridge once existed there is the print of a human foot, three inches deep in the hard rock. Beside it is the mark of a cloven hoof, and there are still stories to be heard of men who were afraid to cross that bridge after dark, and of others, a little braver, who, when doing so, have looked over the railing into the water and seen the reflection of the devil behind their back. The devil, indeed, seems almost as ubiquitous in Wales as he is in Ireland, and it isn't 'all stories of the ignorant peasantry,' for there was the case of a dissenting minister in Denbigh town to whom the fiend appeared 'laughing and grinning at the reverend gentleman behind his back. Only by writing a passage of scripture on a piece of paper, and holding it over his shoulder for the devil to read, could he banish his unwelcome guest.' In our own times a whole parish knows that the devil entered into a dog so that it ran into the vestry and ate the parish accounts. The dog is still alive.

But I don't like to be thinking of hoofs and horns. It's time enough to scratch when you itch. I'd rather reflect on wings and harps and that kind of thing. Don't forget that even if the devil does seem a bit widely domiciled in Ireland, the best harps are Irish too.

Of course the devil has wings, but they are naked as a bat's, and scaly as a dragon's. They are probably slimy, too, and poisonous, like the skin of a toad. I imagine that the points of the spines are sharp, and have barbs on them so that they would give you a nasty tear. But I was thinking of angels' wings.

Have you ever *really* looked at a bird's wing? Have you ever thought of the difference between the short broad wings of birds that inhabit the woods and hedgerows, and the long tapering wings of those who live in the open. The green woodpecker, the jay, and the pheasant dodging through thick cover need something different to the wide-soaring gulls or the zenith-seeking swallows. The wings of a greenfinch are almost as broad as they are long; the average width of a swift's wing is scarcely a quarter of its length. The greenfinch's wing is gently cambered, and its fore-edge is nearly straight; the swift's wing is flat and curved like a scimitar.

And, apart from the manifold shapes, there is the indescribable subtlety of colouring, patches blending with each other to make bars across the forms, light and dark accents pencilling the margin of each feather.

The actual flight of birds differs, too, according to the proportion of their wings to their bodies. A duck whose wings are relatively small must keep up an incessant high rate of flapping if it is to maintain its position in the air. Birds like the starlings and chaffinches with a slightly higher ratio of wing area are able to vary their progress with short glides, though at the cost of some height; hence their undulating flight. But the albatross, the vulture, and the condor, with their great sails spread wide, can soar for hours on end, gaining or losing height according to their least desire.

The soaring of birds is of two kinds, that of the great birds of prey, whose wings are broad as well as long, and richly cambered, and that of the gulls, whose wings are narrow and pointed, and comparatively flat. In the first the birds depend on steeply ascending currents of air, such as occur near mountains and over deserts. In the second they sail almost directly into the wind.

This latter action has been well compared to the 'close-hauled' sailing of a yacht. A keel prevents the yacht being blown to leeward, the weight of the bird has a similar effect in the air. The force of the wind, rising however slightly from the sea, acts on the wing in the same way that the wind, coming from a few points to port or starboard of the bow, acts on the yacht. Some of it thrusts to leeward, some of it escapes astern, the rest impels the yacht or bird forward.

It might be objected that there cannot always be rising currents of air from the sea, yet birds are always soaring; nevertheless it is a very calm day on which there are not 'turbulent airs' above the waves. A ship, too, does not move without causing disturbance in the atmosphere as well as in the sea, and the birds are quick to pick and choose the currents which suit their purpose. We have only to watch them from the deck of a liner to see that every feather on each wing is pulsing the winds. Watch them flying low over the water, how they lift to the air-flow shooting upward from the crest of each wave; watch them at mast height gliding in majestic sweeps, banking, climbing, and seemingly swooning as they drop away to find another air-stream astern.

Even the individual feathers on a wing are miracles. Each one has its main shaft, or quill, from which spring the barbs that form the vanes. Each of these barbs has minute branches called barbules springing from it, and each of these barbules, of which there are about nine hundred and ninety thousand on one primary feather of a pigeon, has microscopic barbicels, sometimes hooked, which interlock and hold the web together. And each feather is perfectly adapted to its purpose. We may think when we see a rook flying that the apparently ragged edges of its wings are due to wear and tear, but if we get a chance to examine a wing we shall find that the first five flight feathers are so shaped that they create those gaps in the wings, gaps which allow the air-stream to pass through and prevent the formation of eddies whose suction would interfere with the flight. The same occurs in many other birds, to a greater or less extent, according to their needs, ranging from the teal, with but two feathers so adapted, to the partridge which has seven. The principle is now used in aeroplane design, where slots in the wings prevent stalling. And that is only one aspect of a few of the many feathers that go to make up a wing.

Have you ever thought as you lay under your eiderdown on a winter's night of the many birds whose breasts have contributed to your comfort—sweet mottle-faced ducks that ride out the coldest storms? Those very feathers now enclosed in silk were once pressed upward against their breasts by hundreds of fathoms of ice-cold water, and the ducks preened them with their serrated bills, smoothing and oiling each plumelet. In early summer they plucked them to line their nests. Don't forget that when those feathers were taken from the nests the eggs were left to be incubated on the frozen ground. Our one consolation may be that the eider will go on laying, again and again, until with luck she succeeds eventually in rearing a brood.

I have heard of a man, he may have been a saint, who never killed a beast for food without first asking pardon of his victim. Perhaps if, in our hearts, we feel the same gratitude toward the ducks all will be well.

CHAPTER ELEVEN

THE HIGH SINGLE-ARCH BRIDGE over the gorge at Rhayader, with its flankings of dilapidated, overhanging houses, is reminiscent of hillside villages in southern Europe. The men of Rhayader are either poets or fishermen, sometimes both. An old man resting on his scythe at the edge of a grass field said to me: 'The burbling of the water is like harp song.' A young man watering his horses said: 'I like to breathe deep, for then all the scents of all the flowers in the valley are mine.' Another, a man with a rod, who was looking at the reflections of a waterfall in a pool a few yards below it, remarked: 'It 's like life; we all reflect the way we 've travelled.'

I was constantly being taken for 'a divine.' I suppose it 's the beard. Every second Welshman that I met told me that I reminded him of his grandfather, who was a great preacher, or of somebody else that afterwards became a bishop or even higher. I think the chief difference between me and an archbishop is that the archbishop is always conscious of sin and I rarely am. That surely can't be due to difference of opportunity! I suppose it 's the way you look at things.

In some parts of the British Isles the vocation of poacher is not held in the highest esteem, but in many parts of Wales it is regarded as a most honourable calling. I know men who are as proud to have the title 'poacher' put after their names on an envelope as any cleric might be to have D.D., or any baronet to have Bart. Like the former it needs close application for a number of years before the award is merited; like the latter heredity has often much to do with it.

A friend of mine with high qualifications told me that when a boy he had the run of the country-side, all but a few acres that belonged to a surly neighbour. Those acres held few birds, yet he got more fun there 'picking a snipe from under the farmer's nose' than in bagging half a dozen grouse on the open mountain. Generally speaking, most of the fun of poaching lies in outwitting the officers of the law. A salmon left on the magistrate's doorstep or a fish hung up outside a pub door so that the bailiff coming out

49

in the dark knocks his head against it are the high lights of the adventure.

It seems to me a very reasonable refinement that a man should pit his intelligence not so much against the innocent dumb beast, bird, or fish, as against one of his own tribe. It is *really* more sporting.

As far as I could gather, poaching round about Rhayader was more a matter of politics than of fish. A lawyer told me that he had seen gangs of two hundred men who were out to kill salmon in order 'to get their own back.'

About a hundred years ago an organization known as 'Rebecca and her daughters' came into being, to deal with the injustices which had arisen in the administration of the turnpike roads. Toll gates were numerous, the tolls had been increased, and in many cases the charges made by the collectors were illegal. Some of the gates had been let to professional renters, who did not scruple to exact the uttermost farthing. Funds, generally, had been mismanaged.

The name of this organization may have been derived from that of an old lady, Rebecca Davies, who kept one of the gates, but it is more generally believed that it had its origin in the story of Isaac and Rebekah, in the book of Genesis, where 'they blessed Rebekah, and said unto her . . . let thy seed possess the gate of those which hate them.' Whatever its source, the practical application of it was that bands of strong men, disguised as women, took the law into their own hands, and went about the country-side at night tearing down and burning the offending barriers. Their activities became so widespread in South Wales that in 1843 a royal commission was appointed to inquire into the matter. It was told me with glee, that on one occasion, while the commission were sitting upstairs, in solemn state, debating the future of dues, duty, tax, etc., 'Rebecca and her daughters' came along, and settled the question, for those particular gates, in no half-hearted manner.

These grievances having been disposed of, the country settled down, but whenever there is any 'trouble' with the law it is to 'Becca' that the country people look for help. Nowadays this applies particularly to fishing.

'We breeds 'em up in these waters,' said a Rhayader man to me. 'Why shouldn't we have one now and again?'

About ten years ago there was misunderstanding between the owners of the fishing and the men who lived beside the river. What it was about I do not know. There must always be a difference of opinion between those who work all day for a few shillings and those who have so much leisure that they have to invent difficulties to make their fishing less effective. The Alexandra fly for trout is now banned on many rivers as being too deadly.

Things came to a head in December of 1932 when 'Rebecca and her daughters' got busy on the Edw, a tributary that joins the main river below Builth. In one night at least eighteen spawn-

ing salmon were killed, and then flashlight photos were taken of the fish and their captors armed with gaffs. The men had disguised their features with burnt cork and cotton wool, for they intended the records to be seen not only by their friends, but by those against whom they had a grudge. They were exhibited in local shops, and even appeared in the newspapers. Proceedings took place before the local bench, but the magistrates considered that the photos did not provide sufficient evidence of identification, and they were compelled to dismiss the cases.

Nowadays a little give and take smooths over many difficulties, and no one makes unpleasant remarks if a salmon spear is seen standing in a corner beside the gun. It may be a very old one, just kept as a curiosity.

It is during floods that fish run upstream, and that reminds me of one day, when the rain that came down on the hills above Rhayader would have made Noah's deluge look like a Scotch mist.

c

I happened to be up on those hills at the time, but before even a drop of water had fallen it was borne in upon me that it would be easy to lose one's way. Indeed, I had already lost it, not once, but several times. Furthermore, I had found a curious track which always led me back to the same place, an uncharted precipice, no matter which way I followed it. I would set my map and compass, and decide that my course lay to the north-east. In twenty minutes I would be peering over the same precipice. Then my compass would tell me that I must strike to the south-west, and in half an hour the same chasm would again be yawning below me. I looked over that cliff at least half a dozen times, and took considerable exercise in the intervals between each survey. Queer things happen in the Welsh mountains.

Then the rain began to fall. The last time I looked over the edge the valley was blotted out. I didn't feel too cheerful.

There are times on the mountains when it is wonderful to be alone, when the last thing that one wants to see or hear is another human being. But there are other times when one thinks of one's widow and orphans. This was one of them. I thought, too, of a big stone carving I'd left unfinished in my studio. It was to have represented Earth; a woman, heroic in size, standing with feet apart, and hands and face upraised to catch the rain. Earth waiting to be fertilized. I remembered how the first time I made drawings for that stone the day had opened fine and clear, so that I was loath to spend the morning indoors, but a friend had offered to pose for me, and I didn't want to lose the opportunity. Friends are so very much more understanding than professional models, whose chief quality is endurance.

The sun was shining brilliantly while I tried to explain my intention. I wanted the arms bent with elbows close to the side, I wanted the head thrown back so that the mass of hair falling over the shoulders would unite with the hands, thereby retaining the solidity of the stone. Rodin once said that a well-designed monument should be capable of withstanding a fall from its pedestal without damage. I wanted my stone to have that quality, no extraneous bits and pieces, essentially a solid block.

I explained all this to my sitter, and I tried to tell her of the thirst of parched earth, as burning and urgent as desire. I wanted her to feel that urgency of thirst, those moments before rain when drought-tormented grasses seem to quiver with expectancy, those moments when birds are silent. Then I wanted her to sense the rain splashing on her face, gathering in small pools in her hair, pouring over her shoulders, streaming from her elbows, shooting from her breasts, coursing the hollows of her thighs. I told her of the broad leaves of tropical plants that act like funnels, guiding the water to their roots. I told her how the growing roots of trees and plants are always where the leaves direct the moisture, close below the stem as in our poplars or in ever-widening circles as in our spreading beeches and oaks.

She stepped on to the throne. Lifting her hands, as I had told her, she threw back her head, and closed her eyes. At that moment there was a burst of thunder, and torrents of giant rain drops split themselves on the window overhead.

This may sound like invention, but it is true. It seemed a good augury then, but something must have gone wrong since, for the stone is still unfinished.

A great many other thoughts went through my head, that day on the mountain; not the least persistent being that I was getting mighty wet. There was no shelter, and even if there had been I might have had to stay there a week before the weather cleared. As I floundered about, dragging my ankles out of soggy bogs, startled sheep would spring from the shelter of a rock or a peat face, frightening me as much as they had been frightened themselves. After following a sheep track up, round, and over what seemed to me like the greater part of mid-Wales, I did eventually reach a wider path, and late in the afternoon I got back to the main road. Then it was three miles home.

By the time I reached the hotel there was a river down my back that would have kept a trout alive, there was enough water in my shoes for a salmon to spawn in, my sketch-book was sodden, I wondered what sort of a lake there was inside my binoculars. A fisherman was standing in the porch of the hotel as I entered. He was looking through the window. 'Nice drop of rain,' he said.

CHAPTER TWELVE

THE TOWN OF BUILTH is some thirteen miles from Rhayader, and whether you walk the river or drive the road the scenery is some of the loveliest on the Wye. The sleek hills and craggy scarps above Rhayader soon give way to rich wooded slopes where, in early summer, the purple of rhododendrons blazes in the fresh green undergrowth. The river varies infinitely. Here deep calm brown water is edged with shining white gravel. There a rushing stream tumbles over successions of shelving rocks, and then sluices through a narrow gorge. In some places where the river bed is wide there seems scarcely a trickle of water, in others where the bed is narrow there is a torrent. Each pool has its name and its associations. Fishermen abound. Between the mouth of the Irfon, a mile below Builth, and the mouth of the Llynfi at Glasbury there is some of the 'most sporting' fishing on the river.

Builth is a modest town, modest in the sense that it is shy and retiring. Until you are close upon it you do not realize that there is a town there at all, its grey roofs being hidden by the surrounding trees. But like many shy and retiring people it has a charm of its own once you are admitted to its intimacies. The streets are narrow and winding, but that is all the better for passing chat. Vehicles of any description seem an intrusion in those streets: they interfere with pedestrians.

It was fair day when I arrived in the town, and I followed the stream of traffic to the fair ground.

'Horse buyers now! Horse buyers, horse buyers! Come on for the ponies now! Come on for the ponies. Eleven of them. Nice little animals, nice little animals. Come on now, the pony buyers!'

The auctioneer, a middle-aged man in a check suit, strode up the alley between the pens of sheep, and cattle, and pigs to where the ponies were confined. Already a dozen or more children were sitting on the railing of the enclosure. The animals were nervous and excited, charging about from side to side of their yard, slithering on its concrete floor as they did so.

'Come on, the pony buyers,' shouted the auctioneer again.

Farmers gathered round. For the most part they wore either hats pulled over their eyes, or caps on the back of their heads. Old mackintoshes covered their shoulders, and with few exceptions brown breeches led the way to black leggings and muddy boots. Each man carried a stick. Some of these were stout and strong, others were slight and tapering and delicately balanced as a rapier. The men of mid-Wales take great delight in a good walking-stick. They will wax lyrical about the golden colour of a hazel or the deep red of a blackthorn. The handles, whittled through many a winter's evening, are rich in character and craftsmanship. Some men are noted for their 'eye for a stick,' others could search all day and not find one. 'Never pass a stick if you see one,' I was told. 'If you do it won't be there when you come back. Cut it out of the hedge when you see it.'

The auctioneer climbed on to the iron railing, and took his seat on the top bar. The owner of the animals stood among them in the pen.

'Now,' said the auctioneer in a confiding tone, 'which will we take first? That's a nice little black mare there, Tom. A fine little mare, that. We'll take her first. There she is, gentlemen, a lovely little yearling mare. We'll take her first.'

Nobody said anything while Tom, the auctioneer's assistant, and the owner of the ponies separated the little black mare from the other ten in the yard.

'There she is now, gentlemen. There she is. Couldn't find a prettier little mare in the country. Lovely little mare, gentlemen! Lovely little mare! She is a mare, isn't she, Tom?' he inquired in an undertone.

Tom made the necessary investigation.

'No, sir. She's a 'orse.'

'A horse, gentlemen, a horse, a lovely little black horse. Couldn't find a prettier little black horse in the country. What'll we say now?　A couple of pounds?　Any one say a couple of pounds?　Come on now, the market's open.　Two pounds, any one give two pounds, lovely little black horse.'

Nobody offered two pounds.

'Well, make an offer, gentlemen.'

Nobody made an offer.

'Any one start with a pound?'

No one would start.

'Come on, gentlemen, lovely little black horse.　Any one start with ten shillings?'

No one would start.

The auctioneer was depressed, but tried not to show it.　'Put him back,' he said to Tom.　'We'll try that grey mare, that one in the corner—there she is going across you—that one there alongside of—no, here she is at my feet.　A lovely mare.　There she is, Mr. Davies, right into your hands,' as the mare thrust her way across the pen once more.　'Now then, gentlemen, what'll we say?　Five year old.　A lovely little mare.　There's her mother beside her, a prize pony.　We're not selling her.　Any one give me three pounds?'

Eventually, with the bidding starting at a pound, she fetched two pounds fifteen.

Then came three ponies, all under a year.　The bidding started at a pound for the three.　It went to twenty-five and then to thirty shillings.　There was a pause and someone bid thirty-one shillings.　'We're not selling rabbits, make it thirty-two and six,' said the auctioneer.　He did.　'Thirty-five.　Thirty-seven and six.　Forty.　Forty shillings for the three ponies.　Come on, Ted, they'd look lovely up on the hill.　Forty-two and six.　Any one make it forty-five?　Forty-five.　Lovely little ponies.　We're not going to send the prices to the paper to-day.　Forty-five shillings.　Any one make it the fifty?　Forty-seven and six. Come on, Mr. Evans.'

Mr. Evans didn't come on, and the ponies were sold for forty-seven and six.

Two mares then fetched five pounds, and that concluded the pony sale, the other animals being withdrawn on account of the low prices.

The auctioneer climbed down from his perch.　The new owner

of the grey mare produced a stick of blue grease paint, spat on it, and drew a broad stripe across the animal's flank. The purchaser of the three yearlings seized each of them in turn and cut their tails off short with a jackknife. Then the gathering dispersed, for there were calves to be sold, and cows with calves, the latter in muzzles, and store cattle.

'There's a grand beast,' said the auctioneer, as a big pure white steer came up for sale.

'No good in the black-out,' said a voice in the crowd.

'He's ready for killing in the daylight,' was the retort.

On all sides animals were being sold, and branded by their new owners. Pigs had various numerals stamped with vermilion on their pink shoulders, and their ears were punctured with pincers. One squeak and it was all forgotten. Cattle, too, had notches punched in their ears. Calves kept arriving, two at a time, in crates on the carriers of private cars. Rams were brought in trailers under rope netting. As often as not the bidding was as mysterious as in a London sale-room. No sign that I could see passed between purchaser and salesman.

On the evening of the next day I met 'Dad.' I'd made friends with his son Owen, who was ploughing on Carneddau Hill, above the town, where I was looking for fossils. Trilobites. I found one too. Owen was interested. He'd seen some of them before, and when I told him that they were casts of an extinct crustacean he very rightly wanted to know how it was that there were so many tails and so few heads. To this I answered that though the animal resembled our wood louse in the way it could curl itself into a ball, it also resembled our lobster in that it shed its hard outer skin many times in the course of its growth. The head being composed of many pieces was likely to become dis-integrated, the tail being shed as one unit left more conspicuous evidence of its existence. I told him that I had seen a specimen, curled up, and so perfectly preserved that, even after hundreds of millions of years, it was still possible, under a magnifying glass, to see the multiple lenses of the eyes. Then we talked of grap-tolites, delicate plume-like fossils that may be found in the slate, and how they had been formed by a creature not unlike a coral polyp, which, in turn, is related to our sea anemones. He took me along to his parents' house to show me one or two specimens that he had found when working in another district. He thought they must be the things I was talking about. Some people had told him they were fairies' pens, but he didn't believe them.

'Dad' had been a miner. He wasn't very interested in fossils. They used to find crystals in the coal seams, white and sharp as dogs' teeth they were, and at one time the miners used to cut them out and bring them to the surface, but the coal-owners thought this led to waste of time, and any man who was caught doing so was promptly sacked. From then on the crystals were treated as irreverently as the rest of the coal.

'Dad' was seventy-three. His head was bald on top, and its sides were close trimmed, but on the near end of his cranium he carried a long grey lock which waved with every breeze. He spoke very little, but his twinkling blue eyes said more than many an eloquent speech. He had a passion for music, in particular *The Barber of Seville*. I hadn't been five minutes in the house before he inquired if I would like him to put it on the gramophone. His daughter changed the subject quickly, but the old man was not to be put off so easily, and at intervals he returned to the charge. His eyes were constantly on the gramophone, and if he and I were left alone for a moment he immediately wandered towards the machine. But he never could get the needle fixed before one of the family returned. Then he would turn aside as if intent on something else.

After the evening meal, which I had been invited to share, he still hovered between the records on the shelf and the machine. There was something sweetly childlike in the way he moved from one to the other, so eager to get a chance to play with his toy. Then for the fourth time he asked me if I liked *The Barber of Seville*, and when I gave him the only answer that was possible he used it to compel permission from his family.

'I tell you what,' said Owen in a tone of the greatest enthusiasm, 'don't put on those first parts, dad, give the orchestra a miss, and cut out the woman's voice. Give us the man's voice on parts six and seven. Squire will like those best.' They had referred to me all the evening, playfully, as 'The Squire.' Apparently I reminded them of some old landowner who 'had the whiskers on him.' As Owen spoke he winked across the room at me.

The old man appeared to agree but, as if by accident, he began with part four. General expostulation compelled him to change it to part five, but even then it was still the woman singing. Finally he put on parts six and seven, playing them through with a rapturous expression on his face.

'That's enough now, dad,' said Owen, letting me see the wink that this time was addressed to his father, as much as to say: 'Our guest isn't really musical, we mustn't bore him.' The old man then pattered off quite happily to amuse himself elsewhere. He had spent forty-eight years of his life underground.

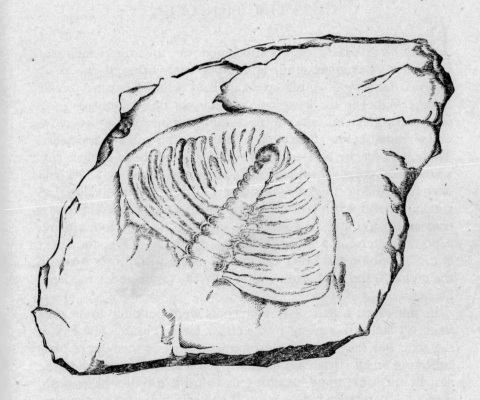

CHAPTER THIRTEEN

BELOW BUILTH the exuberance of the river increases. Hell Hole, Cavaniere Boil, and other such titles of the pools suggest the tempo of the stream. And while the water carves strange shapes in the bare rock of the river bed, man blasts great scars in the green hillsides for the metalling of his roads. Aberedw, a few miles below Builth, is a place of historical importance. There, among the high-terraced rocks, and under an ancient elm, whose roots coil over the rocks like protecting serpents, Llewelyn's cave faces the north-east winds that whistle across the valley. A fringe of hazel scrub hides the rectangular entrance. Within it is cold and damp, not six foot high, and scarcely nine foot square; a poor shelter for a horse, let alone a prince. Over the rocks twine woodbine and other creepers, ferns and primroses grow in the crevices, the wild arum and foxgloves cluster under the hazel bushes.

In mid-April a pair of tree creepers were building among the thick ivy stems that clung to the elm. I was within a few feet of the tree, but they cared little for me. Both of them were busy collecting small sticks and straws. They always approached the nest by the same route, perching first on the top of a hazel bush, then on a particular twig among the purple blossoms of the elm, then on to the ivy about a yard from the nest, finally on to the gnarled stalk which held the nest. Either by design or accident a tuft of sheep's wool had got caught in the bark of the elm, close to the nest, and every now and then, when one of the birds returned with an empty beak it would pull a few strands from this tuft and use it in the building. When the smaller of the two birds, presumably the female, was at work on the inside of the nest, the other one clung to a branch close by, its wings quivering with excitement. The coarse bark of the elm-tree held empty hazel husks, wedged into its crevices by nuthatches before they had rifled the contents.

Long before Llewelyn spent a night in that cave it had been occupied by Saint Cewydd, a brother of Gildas, the historian. The adjoining field has been known for centuries as Cae Cewydd, meaning Cewydd's field, and a few miles away, at Disserth, we find the holy man's name perpetuated at Cilcewydd, which means the church of Cewydd. It was said by one of the early ascetics that though God will bear with the sins of those who live in the world, He will not abide the sins of those who dwell in the desert. I cannot think of many sins which this poor hermit might have committed in that cave, all by himself, but if envy was one—envy of those who might have been living in soft comfort in the valley below—I am sure that a kindly providence would be the first to allow that there were extenuating circumstances. A colder and more miserable place of residence it would be hard to imagine.

Tradition says that Llewelyn, the last Welsh Prince of Wales, spent the night before he was killed in this cave. There are many accounts of his death, but all seem to agree that it happened in the parish of Llanganten, about three miles to the west of Builth, where an obelisk now stands to his memory. There, on a bleak December day in 1282, he met his end, fighting with his followers against the armies of King Edward.

It was not known, at first, that he was among the fallen, but when the soldiers of Sir Edmund Mortimer recognized their foe they severed the head from the body, washed it in the brook near by, and sent it to the king. He, crowning it with a wreath of silver, in derision of Merlin's prophecy that Llewelyn would one day wield the sceptre of Brutus, caused it to be set up in Cheapside.

Wild proud eyes that once held the freedom of the clouds were now shrunken in their sockets. Lips that had loved and been loved hung limp and blue. Locks that had lifted in the wind lay besmeared across a shrivelling forehead. It does not bear thinking about, neither does the treatment accorded to his brother, who was taken prisoner soon afterwards and was tried by a court of eleven earls and one hundred barons. York, Bristol, Winchester, and Northampton were 'honoured' with fragments of this unfortunate man.

Adam of Usk, the early fifteenth-century chronicler, tells us that 'the spring wherein the head of Llewelyn ap Griffith, last Prince of Wales, was washed after that it was cut off, and which is in the village of Builth, throughout a livelong day did flow in an unmixed stream of blood.'

It is generally believed that Llewelyn was betrayed by his armourer. In some accounts we are told that this man, when shoeing the prince's horse, put one of the shoes on back to front, so that its tracks in the snow might be clearly distinguished. In other stories we hear that the smith had been ordered by Llewelyn to put all four shoes on in this way, and that, having obeyed the orders, he sold the information. This misleading device goes back to classical times. There is an old Anglo-Saxon chronicle from which Charles Kingsley drew such an incident in *Hereward the Wake*, and from Virgil and Livy we learn of Cacus, the son of Vulcan, who, having stolen some of Hercules' cattle, dragged them backwards by their tails into a cave so that their rightful owner would never think of looking for them within. Neither would he, indeed, if the imprisoned beasts hadn't set up a hulla-baloo when they heard their old companions lowing outside.

Although in quite a different connection, I cannot help mentioning an ancient Welsh law recorded by Thomas Pennant, who made a tour in Wales in 1773, whereby on complaint that a maiden had been deserted by her lover 'it was ordered by the court, that she was to lay hold of the tail of a bull three years old, introduced through a wicker door, and shaven and well greased. Two men were to goad the beast: if she could by dint of strength retain the bull, she was to have it by way of satisfaction; if not, she got nothing but the grease that remained on her hands.' Pennant goes on to say that 'judging by this and other penalties for the same offence, the crime was not taken very seriously.'

And now we are back again by the Wye, where salmon and trout were leaping before Hercules' father and mother had even begun their courting. In the early morning the shadows of the trout on the bottom of the river are conspicuous, though the trout themselves are difficult to see. A large fly, shining orange in the sunlight, daps up and down to the surface, rising and falling eighteen inches or more. A trout watches it and, each time, as it meets the water, rises but misses. Again and again the fish jumps head and shoulders out of the water, but each time it is too late. The fly flitters behind an overhanging branch, and I am

unable to see the end of the episode. Now a black-backed trout glides from under a patch of weed, turning pale as it pauses over grey shingle. But while I am watching these episodes, a herd of Hereford bullocks has crept up behind me, full of inquiry, sniffing and puffing.

I have a great liking for Hereford cattle. Their big white faces are so childishly innocent. It was a Hereford bull calf that helped me to an extra term at the Slade, when my father said he couldn't afford any more fees.

'If I raise fifteen quid will you do the rest?' I asked.

'I will,' he said, thinking himself safe. He forgot that, a year before, I'd bought a Hereford calf for a pound, and now it was worth eight. I had a pointer bitch, too, Nell was her name, liver and white, and a grand nose. She produced a litter of seven pups, and I sold them at a pound apiece. There was my fifteen pounds, and I went back to the Slade.

One of my father's chief anxieties about my taking up art as a profession was that I would have to draw naked women. I couldn't see anything wrong in that myself. I'll admit, though, that when I did reach the door of the life-room I had a slight quickening of the pulse. That all disappeared when I got inside, for there, on the throne, was the loveliest thing I'd ever seen, pink and white and fresh and natural as the first wild rose of summer. My chief surprise was when she stood up and I realized that women had natural waists. Up till then I had thought 'twas all due to corsets. But that was thirty years ago.

CHAPTER FOURTEEN

SOMETIMES WHEN I WANT to give myself a treat I go along to my friend, Mr. Bottley, in Church Street, Chelsea, and spend a few shillings on a crystal. It may be a green tourmaline from Madagascar, or honey-coloured tinstone from Bolivia, or a golden cluster of pyrites from Elba. The trouble is that I can never keep these crystals for long in my possession. There is something inherent in them which compels me to share them with my friends. I have to pass them on. One day I took a chunk of quartz to a neighbour. It was a big natural crystal, clear and cool as ice, its six facets were smooth as glass, its edges might have been 'machine-finished.'

'My God, Robert, when did you carve that?' he asked, after I had put it on his table.

'I didn't carve it,' I said.

'Well, who did?'

'God carved that,' I told him.

'Well, I 'm damned,' he said, 'wouldn't have thought it possible.'

Of course he spoke without thinking, as so many of us do, but the remark seemed to me singularly expressive of our attitude towards natural phenomena compared with the self-satisfaction we display toward the objects of our own creation. We are astounded at our power to build a dam, but we never think of the water itself as anything approaching a miracle. Water, a liquid so heavy that to lift a bucket of it taxes our strength, is formed of two vapours, and nothing else. That is a fact more staggering than the Elan Valley dams, or even the Panama Canal. Yet the number of charabancs that pass along the metalled roads that bound the reservoirs would put an army of processionary caterpillars (see Fabre, *Souvenirs entomologiques*, series VI) into the shade, and passengers on ships lean over the rails in open-mouthed astonishment at the machinery and concrete walls of the locks at Miraflores and Gatun. They did not leave their deck chairs to wonder at the Pacific Ocean which they have just left, neither will they do so to contemplate the Atlantic which they are about to enter. Meals and exercise may compel them to move, but not the almost

65

unfathomable depths of clear, buoyant, teeming waters, singing
and swelling to every change of moon.

I would like to write a homily on the moon, but beyond its
power, on occasion, of obliterating mental equilibrium I know
nothing. On the other hand the fact that light, which travels at
the rate of seven and a half times round our world in a second,
has not yet reached us from countless unknown stars seems to me,
if not humiliating, at least mildly sedative.

There is no shortage of natural phenomena to wonder at beside
a river. Every stone has a history that makes the grandest item
in *Debrett* look silly. Every leaf, from its unfolding to its fall, is
a seasonal repetition of a phantasmagoria of cellular activity more
weird and incomprehensible than our wildest imaginings. Every
animal we see demonstrates the amazing power of that fragment
of the reproductive cell which determines hereditary characteristics.

In a male rabbit that reproductive cell is but one ten-thousandth
of a millionth of the rabbit's body, and the 'gene,' or heredity-
determining factor, is but a *fragment* of that cell, nevertheless it
controls not only all the characteristics which make a rabbit a
rabbit and not a hare, a fox, or any other animal, but also the
essentials of size, colour, temper, and other attributes which the
young rabbit shall inherit from its parent.

Tastes differ. Voices differ. Our powers of appreciating
scents differ. It is all due to the microscopic 'gene.' The children
of parents, both of whom are unable to appreciate the taste of any
particular food, will also be unable to find any relish in that same
dish. We are told that a marriage between a soprano and a basso
can only produce offspring with soprano or bass voices, and that
the union of a tenor and an alto can only give children with
similar voices. On the other hand, if a man with a baritone voice
should wed a lady who sings mezzo-soprano they should, if they
so desire, have a reasonable chance of producing a quartet.

Dr. Albert Blakeslee, of the Carnegie Institute in Washington,
made experiments with over eight thousand visitors to the International Flower Show in New York in 1935. He found that,
though the same flower might have a strong scent for one person
and a weak scent for another, that would not be on account of any
general difference between the two people's sensibility, for the
reactions of those same two people might be completely reversed

before a different flower. He found too that 'what was described by one as a delicious perfume might be characterized by the next as an intolerable stench.' He tells of a woman who, confronted with two bowls of freesias, of different varieties, insisted that the whole affair was foolish. 'Everybody knows that freesias have a lovely odour, and to ask if freesias are fragrant is a silly question. It was suggested that she try the two varieties on the table herself, and notice for a while how others voted. She started with the "A" flower, and turned on us indignantly. "There is something the matter with these flowers, they don't smell at all! You have done something to them." She was assured that they had not been doctored in any way. As she put her nose down among the "B" flowers, her features relaxed, and with a smile she exclaimed: "A perfectly heavenly odour." While she waited watching the other visitors, a man approached the "A" flowers, which she had been unable to smell, and called them strong. Upon smelling the "B" flowers, which the woman had called heavenly, the man's features hardened, and he turned to the attendant almost with anger and said: "Lady, these stink, they stink like hell." The objecting woman's face flushed, and she left the group without further objections.'

The same scientist tells us that in his garden there was a pink-flowered verbena and a red-flowered verbena, and that of about forty people who sniffed those plants two-thirds could perceive fragrance in the pink flowers, but none in the red, while the other third could smell fragrance in the red but not in the pink.

Meanwhile the rivers burble on, and the sedges and the rushes, bending in the wind, care not a hoot for ideas of any kind.

About a mile to the south-west of Builth there is a brook called Nant-yr-Arian, or 'Money Brook.' It acquired its name at the time of the plague, when the country people brought there the produce they had for sale, and the townspeople in order to avoid spreading contagion dropped their money, in payment, into the brook.

At Llanelwedd, across the main river from the town, the present vicarage was formerly an inn. There, once a year, 'The Fancy' collected to decide the cock-fighting championship of Hereford-shire, Radnorshire, and Breconshire. According to Welsh rules thirty-two birds were put into the pit at the same time, and sixteen pairs would begin to fight. When any bird was defeated it was withdrawn by its owner until eventually but two remained. Great was the excitement when these finalists met in mortal combat.

'All that is over now.' So I was told, but here and there about the country-side, and in the back yards of town houses, one may come across game-birds, cared for like racing greyhounds. 'We don't fight them any longer,' one owner said to me, 'but we like to keep the sport alive,' whatever he meant by that. Pointing out one resplendent cock, he added: 'That bird was left to me by the Reverend Owen Morgan. Seventy-eight, he was, when he died. "All my birds to Pugh" were his last words.'

In Tudor times, at Cregrina, a few miles to the east of Builth, the last wolf to be killed in South Wales met its end. Whether it was actually the last of its kind in the district we cannot tell. It may have left a mate to roam, solitary, about the hills until, unable any longer to run down its prey, haggard, mangy, and toothless, it slunk into a cave and died; the last of a race that had inhabited the country for as long, probably, as man himself.

Before leaving Builth I must quote the Reverend Theophilus Jones who, writing in 1809 of the parish of Llanganten, says: 'Upon entering the church it resembles an ill swept barn, or at least so it appeared to me, but that it might not be mistaken for a building of that description, I observed at the west end a small bell hung up and a rope appendant to it, while below was a *memento mori* not painted or daubed on the wall, as too common in country churches, but taken *after the life*: in plain English, one or two human skulls were thrown upon the ground with apparent inattention, but perhaps designedly to remind the thoughtless stranger that he was near a place of interment, and to inspire the audience during the time of divine service with greater awe and devotion: the seats and benches are here miserably decayed and broken: what is called the communion table is couped up like a small pew without a door, so that a stall fed prebendary can hardly turn round, though a lean curate may perhaps squeeze himself into it.'

This description would not apply to-day. The church is as spick and span as any in Wales, and there is ample room for prebendary, curate, and, if need be, bishop behind the rails.

CHAPTER FIFTEEN

THEY ARE ALL POETS in Wales. I overtook an old man on the road as he was carrying two buckets of water from the village well. He was moving slowly, as if he was conscious of their weight, so I offered to carry them for him.

'The storm has passed over,' he said.

'Are you taking them far?' I asked.

'The storm has passed over,' he answered again, and then, as if as an afterthought, he added, 'and I haven't far to go.'

He put the buckets on the road and stood beside them. He didn't look up. His mind seemed abstracted, his thoughts seemed far away. Then he began to speak. 'I watched him grow like a young green shoot: every year of his life was like a leaf unfolding. But the storm has passed over, and the flower is broken at the root. The oak-trees and the firs on the hills are borne down under the weight of the ice that is on them. They are no colder than my heart. The one branch that was left to me is fallen.'

As he bent to lift the buckets I took them from him and carried them as we walked along. 'Is it your son that you 've lost?' I asked.

'My son is gone from me this fifteen years. He died, and his wife followed soon after, and then I reared their boy. The neighbours tried to take him from me, but I wouldn't let him go. I could dry his clothes as well as another. When he was sick I could nurse him. I wouldn't let him go to strangers. He didn't want to go. There was only the two of us in the house. But he 's gone now, and I haven't far to go. Forty years I 've carried the water all but one day, the day he nearly left me, a dozen years ago. Eight years old, he was. "Hold my hand, grandsir," he said. That was all he said, all the day through. "Hold my hand, grandsir." I couldn't go to fetch the water. And now they have split the lovely chest that was on him, the lead has pierced through him, the blood has gone from him. There was a lone swan passed over the house at dawn. I never felt the weight in them buckets until to-day.'

When we reached his yard he asked me to leave the water there.

'You are a big man, and the strength is still in you, and you have far to travel.'   He pushed the iron gate open and carried his burden through.   'I haven't far to go now,' he said.

When I passed through the village a week later they were burying 'Old Gwynne.'

CHAPTER SIXTEEN

WALES WAS ALWAYS NOTED for its cattle, and the wealth of the country lay to a considerable extent in those cattle. As an example of this we have a letter, written in 1674 by Sir Roger Mostyn to his neighbour Piers Pennant:

'DEAR PYERS,

'I hope you will excuse me for asking for the £4 you owe me for the pair of oxen, but I want the money to make up £20 to send my son to Oxford next week. . . .'

The great majority of the beasts sent to England during the sixteenth and seventeenth centuries were black, though as early as the fifteenth century there were red cattle with white faces in Glamorgan. Until towards the end of the nineteenth century, when railway facilities became available, it was the custom to drive them in great droves along the highways, or wherever possible over the 'green roads,' in order to avoid the all-too-frequent toll-gates. It was common in those days, and it must have been impressive, to see long lines of great jet steers labouring in single file along these mountain tracks so that it might have been the crest of the hill itself that was moving, were it not for an occasional horseman that broke the skyline. From Carmarthenshire, Pembrokeshire, and Cardiganshire thousands upon thousands of these cattle would plod their way to the fairs and markets of England. To Leicester, Northampton, and London, even to Essex and Kent they would go, moving at a steady twenty miles a day.

Rhydspence, a few miles below Hay, was an important halt on the long journey. The fourteenth-century inn still stands, its walls thick with black beams, its roof of heavy tiles sparkling with patches of yellow stonecrop. Till recently it was known as the Cattle Inn. Here it was that 'the creatures' were shod before setting out on the hard roads of England. Two light slippers to each hoof meant eight shoes to each animal. Many if not all of them would have been shod before they started on the trek, the work being often done by itinerant blacksmiths, but by the time they reached the border their hoofs would need attention. Men worked hard in those days. There is on record an instance where two smiths, with their two assistants, set out from Bala to Dolgelly, eighteen miles away, leaving their home at three o'clock in the morning, and carrying with them four hundred and eighty ox shoes, with the necessary nails and implements. On arrival they set to work and shod sixty bullocks 'between two and a half and three years old, and hard to throw,' and in the evening walked the eighteen miles back to Bala.

For the convenience of dealers and drovers a number of private banks became established in Wales, each of which issued its own notes. At Llandovery there was the Bank of the Black Ox, whose promises to pay were decorated with an engraving of a black ox. At Aberystwyth there was the Bank of the Black Sheep, with black sheep on the notes corresponding to the number of pounds for which the paper was valued. A black lamb was the emblem on the ten-shilling note.

Besides cattle, Welsh ponies, three or four hundred at a time, might be met on the road. Geese too, in enormous flocks, and, strange to relate, shod. The method of shoeing was the same as that employed in Germany when fat geese were driven long distances to the markets, the birds being compelled to walk through alternate layers of tar and sand until their unfortunate feet had accumulated an impasto which would protect them on their arduous march. Turkeys were once dealt with in the same way in Norfolk.

I am sorry for cattle. They are such amiable creatures. I love their wet muzzles, their scent, their childlike simplicity. Bullocks are treated most shamefully when they are young, and heifers are only respected for their possibilities of milk yield. It is a terrible responsibility that the average man in this country consumes in his lifetime the equivalent of about six full-grown cattle, twenty-five sheep, and fifteen pigs. Heaven only knows how many birds he lays hands on, each one infinitely more pleasant to look upon than himself. Compare the attire of the cock pheasant with that of the field marshal who shoots him. Even granting the latter the glory of full dress, there isn't a single item of the whole tawdry outfit that could compete with the living glory of a pheasant's breastplate. I am not suggesting for a moment that we should all turn vegetarian; I am only asking that we should realize our responsibility in this matter. It is one of the liabilities that came to us with reason. There is a price for everything in this world, even for the taking of life. The honest man does not run into debt.

There is no shortage of ruined castles in the border country between Wales and England, but many of these ruins are so dilapidated that there is little of them to be seen. At Rhayader nothing is left but the fosse, and that now makes a convenient rubbish dump for the town. It seems, however, that the building was never of anything more substantial than wood, and that Llewelyn the Great took full advantage of that when, in 1215, he set fire to it. Nothing has been heard of it since then. At Builth there are fragments of a Norman castle. At Maesllwch there is a nineteenth-century version of an ancient building. At Hay there is a gateway and tower of another Norman castle to which was once added 'a handsome Jacobean house.' Fortunately, that has since been burnt down. The Norman castle appears to have been built during the reign of Henry I but, according to legend, it was rebuilt in King John's reign by a lady known as 'Maud Walbee,' who was the wife of one William de Breos, a descendant of Philip de Breos, who had come over from Normandy with the Conqueror. Maud was described as 'malapert and stomachful,' which, I suspect, means that she was possessed of a sharp tongue. She very unwisely accused King John, to his face, of murdering his nephew Arthur, for which temerity she was walled up and starved to death. Tradition says that she was also possessed of supernatural powers, and that she built Hay Castle in one night, carrying the stones in her apron from a quarry some miles away. One of these stones, a mere pebble nine foot long, fell into her shoe, whereupon, finding it uncomfortable, she threw it across the Wye into Llowes churchyard, where it stands to this day towering in dignity over everything else in the churchyard. It is now generally believed that the stone is an ancient menhir, and that the Celtic crosses carved on either side are comparatively recent additions; that, in fact, the stone is but one of the many pagan memorials converted to Christian uses which are to be found both at home and abroad.

A few miles below Hay the ruins of Clifford Castle stand high over the river.   Many a time, no doubt, the daughter of the house, Jane Clifford, must have looked up and down that river debating in her mind the rival claims of an uninspiring knight who offered her his name and a king who offered her his love.   Wisely, I think, she chose the latter, and if she did die young as a result of her choice she held the love of her man, and that a king, to the end.   Does any woman ask more?

Nowadays thistles and yellow loosestrife carpet the ground where once sweet sedges were strewn, and, in place of heraldic blazonings and armour, wallflowers and wild roses decorate the walls.   It would not be difficult to build up a picture of the life once lived within those castle walls with its grandeur and display, its intrigues and petty jealousies, but I prefer to think of Fair Rosamund slipping away from the assembled company, as she often must have done, to the little lake near by now known as Leich's Pool.   She may have had some special confidante who would have gone with her.   They would have had to pick their skirts high when crossing that boggy land, and no doubt they squealed when they sank ankle deep in the squelching mud.   I can see the two of them sitting under an ancestor of the oak-tree that now leans over the pool while they dried their pink feet and watched the moorhens sailing across the pond with their tails cocked up like the sterns of Spanish galleons.   They would have watched the dabchicks too, bobbing up and down among the water-lilies, watched the wild duck lead her brood from clump to clump of rushes, and pondered on the simplicity of the loves of birds and the complexity of the loves of man.   Then with posies of willow herb, wild mint, and bogbean they would have crept back to the castle and been soundly rated by some old duenna, who, remembering her own youth, didn't mean a word of what she said.

But if castles are numerous they are nothing to relics of an earlier civilization.   There can hardly be a hill in Wales on which you cannot scratch your back against a monolith or a cromlech if you feel so inclined.   The ordnance map is dotted with them. One of the most striking of these is known as Arthur's Stone, at Dorstone.   Some say it is Thor's Stone, and that the name of the village is taken from it.   It stands high on the hill, a wide circle of upright slabs surrounding others which support a capstone close on twenty feet in length and more than half that at its widest.

Before I climbed the hill from Bredwardine I dropped into the old church by the bridge, to see the alabaster figure of the Sir Robert Vaughan who, with Davy Gam, was killed at Agincourt. He is said to have been the original of Fluellen in Shakespeare's *Henry V*. It is a fine effigy, and it ought to have aroused 'great thoughts' within me; so ought the ancient building itself, whose

ground plan is so irregular that many of the congregation sitting in the pews at the west end are unable to see the east window or the altar. But even the grotesque Norman carvings seemed of little interest. My one desire that day was to get out of the valley and away from the innumerable hordes of flies that infested it.

I often think how tenuous is the thread that holds our thoughts together. Hunger, thirst, heat, cold, a touch of any of them and all the aesthetic and philosophic thoughts on which we pride ourselves vanish as by a wand. For most people a mere flea inside the shirt can ruin Beethoven.

It is a stiff climb up the hill to the cromlech, and the day that I made that journey seemed to be the hottest day of the year. But my toil was relieved by the company of an old man who overtook me while I was watching a green woodpecker. Stockeagle, he said, was what they used to call it in those parts, and Blue Isaac was what they called the hedge-sparrow. He didn't know why. It might be the colour of the eggs. He was 'certain sure' of the name. He was going to see his son-in-law who was ill, having the sickness for his wife, who was with child. Why, yes, it often happened. Indeed, he knew of a case where a man who wasn't even married to a girl was ill every morning. That proved he was the father.

Though such sympathy between two people may be rare it is happily less rare than the practice of wife-selling, which existed well into the nineteenth century, and was accepted as lawful by the local authorities. In the *Hereford Times* for 20th May 1876 we read the following from a correspondent: 'I must recall to your memory my statement as to my being playfellow to Mona Delnotte Coates, for it was while out walking with her and her attendant that I first saw a man selling his wife. We were going from the Barton to the other side of the town, and necessarily had to pass the bottom of the pig market. Here we saw a crowd. The girl was desirous of knowing what was the matter, so she elbowed her way through the people, and was followed by the children to the open space in the centre. There stood a woman with her hat in her hand. All classes of women wore hats then very much like those worn now, only as artificial flowers were then very dear, they were covered all over the tops with massive bows, and sometimes had a plume of feathers. This woman's hat was a very smart one. She stood looking down. At first I thought she was admiring her own red cloak, but as she stood so still my eye wandered over to see what was amiss; and I shall never forget how surprised I felt when I observed she had a rope about her neck, and that a man was holding one end of it. "What has she done?" we both cried out, for I believed she was going to be hanged. "Oh," said a bystander, "she has done no good, depend upon it, or else he wouldn't want to sell her." Just then there was a loud laugh and a man shouted: "Well done, Jack, that is eleven pence more than I would give; it's too much boy, too much." But Jack stood firm. "No," said he, "I'll give a shilling, no more, and he ought to be thankful to get rid of her at any price." "Well," said the man, "I'll take it, though her good looks ought to bring more than that." "Keep her, master, keep her for her good looks," shouted the laughing bystanders. "No," said he, "good looks won't put the victuals on the table without willing hands." "Well," said Jack, "here's the shilling, and I warn't I'll make her put the victuals on the table for me, and help to get it first; be you willing, missis, to leave him and take me for better or worse?" "I be willing," said she. "And be you willing to sell her for what I bid, master?" "I be," said he, "and will give the rope into the bargain." So Jack gave the man his shilling, and the man put the rope into Jack's hand and Jack walked off up the pig market leading his newly bought wife by the halter.'

The writer goes on to say that she knew them all through their lives afterwards, and the woman worked hard to help her husband in his trade of weaving. She also relates how she saw several other women sold in a similar way on other occasions, though they did not seem so willing to make the change. The custom wasn't confined to Herefordshire. At Birmingham on 31st August 1773 a woman was sold in open market for one shilling. At Sheffield, in the year 1796, a similar case occurred, and there a toll of fourpence was charged by the market toll collector.

By 1826 the price seems to have risen. At Brighton in that year a wife fetched thirty shillings with a toll of one shilling. The toll collector in this case was challenged by the magistrates as to his right to make such a charge. He replied by quoting from the market by-laws: 'Any article not enumerated in these by-laws pays one shilling.'

But these are sad stories. Let us think of something more cheerful. Here is a recipe for potato wine that I gleaned from an old lady in a cottage near Monnington a few miles further down-stream:

'Fower punds a taters to a gallon a watter. They mun be owld taters, um munna be new, owld uns, like, as from summer a twelve-month gone. Bile um till um be done, but dunna thee 'low th' skins t' crack. If a waants wine a bit stronger, like, put a bit a whe-ut in th' brew afore bilin'. When th' taters be biled propur, power th' watter through a bit a muslin int' a stean, and leave it t' coo-ul. When it be propur coo-ul, put some brewers' barm, what um do call yeast, in it to wark it. Dunna thee mix the barm wi' nowt but cowld watter. It wunna wark wi' watter as 'as bin biled. Then put in sugar, fower pund t' th' gallon disackly it 'll waant, and leave it t' wark fur three days, mebbe fower. Have a look at it twice a day, and skim the scum off as it rises t' th' top. When no more scum comes t' th' top, strain int' bottles, and it sh'd be in right farm fur drinkin' in six months.'

CHAPTER SEVENTEEN

THE WYE DIVIDES ITSELF naturally into three sections, the first from its source to Boughrood, a few miles above Hay, where it is all the time a torrent tumbling joyously from the hills, whispering, sighing, singing in the shallows, tossing tumultuous at the falls, seething and swirling in the pools; the second where it winds calm and leisurely through the wide valley whose soil is red as the flesh of salmon; the third after Goodrich when with accumulated energy it cuts its way through one majestic gorge after another until, finally, joining its sister the Severn, it gently merges into the sea.

I had followed the whole watercourse on foot until I reached Three Cocks, which is just below Boughrood. I had travelled slowly and sedately as any old heron, peering into rapids, pondering over pools, and straying but short distances from the river bank when it became necessary to seek the wherewithals of life. But at Three Cocks the weather became so bad that my progress for a time was more like the long flying leaps of those giant antediluvian creatures, half reptile, half bird, that once floundered where we now grow our spuds and roses. I must confess, too, that hereabouts the inhabitants seemed to be rather more property-conscious than by the upper reaches. Some of the fences might have been international boundaries. Indeed, I have crossed from France into Spain with far greater ease than I negotiated some of the barriers between riverside properties. Of course it may be that the rich soil of the alluvial meadows is better worth guarding than the bracken-covered slopes of the hills. There's generally a good reason for local as well as racial characteristics and the people themselves are seldom to blame. One cannot expect the inhabi-

78

tants of our big manufacturing towns, who must ever speak
against the clanging of machinery, to have the softness in their
voices of those who live on the seaboard of the Atlantic, and tune
their words to the winds and to the waves. One cannot expect
diamond merchants to store their goods in the open as coal
merchants do. Even so a combination of thorns, barbed wire,
brambles, and nettles is discouraging.

But at the old coaching inn, the 'Three Cocks,' they have comfortable beds, and they know how to cook potatoes so that they

partake of the quality of flour rather than of soap, and they understand the aesthetic as well as the gastronomic qualities of a dish
piled high with tender green peas.[1] They know, too, the value
of boiled salmon to a growing man, so I stayed there for some
days, and during the one short break in an otherwise continuous
downpour I visited Llangorse Lake, a stretch of water some five
miles in circumference.

This lake is also known as Savadden, and in a Harleian MS. of
about 1695 we read that: 'In the greate Poole call'd Llyn Savathan
once stood a faire citie which was swallowed up in an Earthquake
and resigned her stone walles into this deep and broad water,
being stored most richly with fish in such abundance as is un-
credible . . . and indeed the fishermen of this place have often

[1] On reading this, my publisher, an otherwise cultivated gentleman, with exquisite
taste in literature, writes: 'But *I* [the "I" heavily underlined], like Edward Bunyard
and other gastronomes, *prefer* ["prefer" also underlined] soapy spuds. You should
try the Austrian Kipfler, or the French Belle de Juillet—fried, of course.' Readers
will, I am sure, excuse further comment.

times taken up goodes of severall sortes from the very harte of the Poole but whether these might be goodes that ware cast away is unknowne but we have never heard of any such mischance in oure times.' The story is probably derived from the remains of ancient lake dwellings which have been identified on an island on the north side of the lake. This island, wholly artificial, was connected with the shore by a causeway of stones and piles, with probably a drawbridge. On it have been discovered the bones of red deer, wild boar, and cattle.

It is told, to-day, that when the lake is rough the buried church bells can be heard ringing under the water. When I asked a man who had his dwelling by the lake if he had ever heard the bells he replied 'bunkum.' When I asked him if it was true that the waters of the river Llynfi, which enter the lake, do not mix with the lake water, but flow through unstained, he replied 'bunkum.' When I asked him if the lake was not celebrated for its miracles he replied 'bunkum,' and with that amount of information I reached home before the next downpour.

The Black Mountains rise up sharp to the west of Llangorse, and at the head of the Honddu valley is Capel-y-ffin (The Chapel at the Boundary). It is there that not long ago they tried to lay a ghost by turning the dead man in his grave, but after they had turned him 'he came back seven times worse.' Close to the chapel is Llanthony Abbey, built by an Anglican clergyman, self-styled Father Ignatius, towards the end of the nineteenth century. A few miles down the valley stand the far more imposing ruins of the priory, built by Augustinian monks in the twelfth century. In recent times Eric Gill lived at the abbey for a few years, and it is certainly as cold a spot as any anchorite could wish for. I can still remember the dinners by candlelight at the long refectory table, every one wearing overcoats or shawls, while members of Gill's family took it in turn to read the Epistle and Gospel for the Day and a chapter from the *Martyrology*. But if the stone floors were cold, hearts were warm; Eric was as lovable a man as you could meet.

I hope it will not hurt anybody's feelings if I tell how a favourite saying of his, 'The artist does the work, the critic gets the in-spiration,' came to be realized in one of his own pieces of sculpture. At the time that he was working on the large torso, which afterwards became known as 'Mankind,' his studio in London was near to mine, and I used to visit him nearly every day.   I saw the great column of stone, some eight or nine feet high, before ever he touched it with a tool, and he told me then that his only idea about it was to carve the largest female torso that he could get out of the stone.   He said that he didn't want to be bothered with head, arms, and legs, he just wanted to enjoy carving a body which would represent his ideal of feminine beauty.   Under his instructions, then, his mason worked until he himself took over with hammer and punch.   Soon it was possible to see the rough outline of the huge figure.   Then the punch gave way to the claw which was to carry it all a stage further, in readiness for the final carving with the chisel.   I remember that, in his eagerness to see some part of the stone finished, he went ahead with the chisel before he had finished all over with the claw, so that at one time there were three different states to be seen: the deep ridges, encircling the forms, from the punch, the 'combed' surface from the claw, and the smooth stone almost polished by his amazing skill with the chisel.   It was at this stage that he shocked two somewhat puritan visitors by telling them, when they remarked on the hardness of the work, that in reality it was great fun.   It was like undressing a girl, he said, each layer of stone a garment, first one got rid of the rough woollies, finally the delicate silk.   Eric liked these little innocent naughtinesses.

One day when I was with him he told me that he was worried about the thighs of the torso, which at knee height stuck rather awkwardly into the supporting base.   He felt that whereas such abruptness in a classical torso, mutilated by time, was entirely reasonable, the same thing carved deliberately would be lacking in design and less acceptable.   While we debated the question, viewing the work from all angles, I noticed that his mason had for the time being allowed a quantity of stone to remain behind the knees, to give the figure greater strength, while it was being carved.   'Why not make it a kneeling torso?' I suggested. 'There's plenty of stone there, and it will give more of an architectural base to the figure.'   Eric thought this was a good idea. It would be something new and 'rather fun.'   Next day when I went to see him he had roughed it out as I had suggested, and the alteration seemed to solve his problem.

In due course the carving was finished, and in due course it went to his exhibition at the Goupil Gallery. 'What is the title?' he was asked.

'Blowed if I know,' said Eric, or words to that effect.

'It seems to me,' said a lady with mystic leanings, who was in the gallery, 'like a symbol of mankind kneeling to God.'

'Well, call it "Mankind,"' said Eric. So it was named 'Mankind' in the catalogue, and its symbolism has since inspired many writers.

But in this respect Eric is in good company. A similar story is told of Rodin. It seems that one morning the sculptor had wrestled not only with a recalcitrant idea, but with a recalcitrant model, until in desperation he told the man to go. The model, as irritated as Rodin, strode across the floor of the studio, gesticulating about the pose. Rodin, noticing a particular movement, shouted at him to 'hold the pose.' All his models were trained to do this at any instant. Then quickly, in his usual way, the sculptor threw together small bits of clay, which caught the action. He felt better when he had done that. It was utterly unlike what he had been searching for all the morning, but that didn't matter. There *was* something there. He told the model to come back later.

A few moments afterwards a friend calling to take the artist to lunch found him contemplating a tiny figure in wet clay of a naked man striding forward with one hand pointing upwards and the other pointing to the ground.

'Hallo,' he asked, 'John the Baptist?'

Rodin thought for a moment. Then he answered 'Yes.' But what really interested him was the movement of the figure, what he himself called 'une sorte d'évolution entre deux équilibres.'

I have no doubt that in one way or another the same has happened to many other artists. To find a title is often much more difficult than to paint the picture.

We all know the old tag that art is not inspiration but perspiration. Blake, when looking through one of Constable's sketch-books, exclaimed with enthusiasm: 'Why, this is not drawing, but inspiration.' Constable replied: 'I never knew it before; I meant it for drawing.' Turner, when pressed to speak at the fashionable gatherings of his day, would merely reply that painting was a 'rum go.'

CHAPTER EIGHTEEN

I MENTIONED A SPIRIT that, in recent times, would not be laid, at Capel-y-ffin. Writing in 1780 the Rev. Edmund Jones tells of a woman, 'a true experimental Christian beyond many,' who saw 'one of the Dogs of hell coming hastily on to meet her, but being come within four or five yards of her, and it was well he came no nearer, it stopt, sat upon its backside and set up such a scream, so horrible, and so loud and strong, that the earth moved under her, and that she thought the hill was rent by it. . . .'

The same author tells of a maid-servant who was greatly troubled by an evil spirit which 'in winter pulled the cloaths from her bed: in summer piled additional cloaths upon her,' and of a woman who saw a bowl of fire skipping along the road before her out of which came forth flames about half a yard long. From Breconshire comes the story of a female spirit which carried a young man 'to and from Philadelphia over the vast Atlantic Sea and much land' in a space of three days and three nights, in order that he might find a box 'in which was two hundred pounds in half-crowns,' and drop it into the sea. 'When he came home he could hardly speak'— I don't blame him—'and his skin was somewhat like leather,' which is no wonder, indeed. The author in accounting for this says: 'Disembodied Spirits are vastly stronger out of the body than they can possibly be in it because it is a load about the spirit which greatly hinders its operation.' They seem to be better educated, too, for there was one, in Scotland, who corrected the minister's Latin when he replied to her utterances.

But it isn't only unhappy or unfriendly spirits that we hear of. There was the case of John Jones, who, when in danger of being murdered on the moors near Machynlleth, found himself accompanied by a handsome stranger, on a grey horse, who disappeared when the danger was over. There was another spirit that would attach itself to individuals, and work hard for them provided they played no tricks on him. If anything like that happened he would quickly take his revenge and vanish. Other well-disposed ghosts have come along and pointed out where money was hidden. Another, remembering the past, and wishing either to repeat it

D

or to make amends for wasted opportunities, appeared at one time as a man who kissed girls in the dark, and at the next as a beautiful woman asking to be kissed.

Equally strange, the Rev. Francis Kilvert, writing in his diary on 5th January 1878, notes that in the village of Staunton-on-Wye at midnight on Christmas Eve an old man saw the oxen that were standing kneel down upon their knees and those that were lying down rise up on their knees, and 'there they stayed kneeling and moaning, the tears running down their faces.' This was a common superstition in many parts of England and Wales. Thomas Hardy in his poem on Christmas Eve, entitled *The Oxen*, writes:

> 'We pictured the meek mild creatures where
>   They dwelt in their strawy pen,
> Nor did it occur to one of us there
>   To doubt they were kneeling then.'

In places it was believed that death would soon overtake any one who stayed up to see the animals on their knees.

Elsewhere in the diary Kilvert tells of the Rev. John Price, 'a solitary,' who became vicar of Llanbedr-Painscastle in 1859. But Mr. Thoresby Jones has given us a more picturesque description of the old man. In his *Welsh Border Country* he writes: 'The stipend was meagre, and there was no vicarage: Price lived in three old bathing machines, which served respectively as study, bedroom, and kitchen. After these were accidentally burnt down he dwelt in a brick and slate hen-house. The parishioners, mostly dissenters, did not find their way to church. Interpreting literally the parable of the Marriage Feast, he went out to the highways and hedges to procure guests for his spiritual banquet; and soon an offer of sixpence per head per service began regularly to fill his pews with unwashed tramps and their draggle-tailed doxies. Later, when he lost a tiny private income, this had to be reduced to fourpence. This new proposal was solemnly discussed in the churchyard, and finally accepted by a sort of informal Tramps' Union. For the comfort of his flock in winter he provided oil stoves; cooking was allowed during the sermon. Price further offered five shillings to each pair of vagrants "living in sin" who would consent to let him join them in Holy Wedlock. As his sight was very weak, several business-like couples let him marry them half a dozen times. Having sunk into a very neglected state, he was taken by friends to Talgarth, where it was found necessary to cut his clothes off his skin. He did not survive the bath which followed.'

Kilvert spent the last years of his life at Bredwardine, on the opposite side of the river from Staunton, and among other poems which he wrote was one entitled *Welcome Home*, the theme being the tolling for a funeral of the bells at Bredwardine Church, this being done in a particular way, and known locally as 'The Welcome Home.'

Bells, the longest lived of all musical instruments, have, almost universally, in man's fancy, been endowed with personality. They are given affectionate names, such as Great Harry of Canterbury, Old Kate of St. Mark's at Lincoln, Great Peter at York, and of course Big Ben in London, and their music is regarded almost as a personal call, whether it be to sorrow or rejoicing. After Trafalgar, when the nation's jubilation for victory was tempered by its mourning for Nelson, the joy peals from the tower of Chester Cathedral were sobered by intermittent strokes from a single muffled bell. In the churchwardens' account for St. Benedict's of Lincoln we find the following items among many others of a similar nature:

1685.	May 29th.	Paid for ye bell, King Charles Restoration	1	6
1718.	Nov. 5th.	Paid for ringing ye bell for Guy Fawkes		6
1759.	Oct. 25th.	Paid for ringing for Quebec	1	0
1761.	July 14th.	Paid for ringing when beating the French	1	0

In past times, too, the Seeding Bell, the Harvest Bell, the Gleaning Bell called labourers to their work; the Oven Bell gave notice when the lord of the manor's oven had been heated and was ready for his tenants' dough.

In Herefordshire, as elsewhere, the peals of the bells from various churches have been translated into jingles, some of which throw sidelights on local history. The fact that at Staunton-on-Wye folk declare that the bells at Norton Canon say,

> 'Norton's men be hungry,
> Stole a pig last Monday,'

suggests that there had been some slight friction between these neighbouring villages. Norton's men preserve a dignified silence on the subject.

'Bim Boum, Bim Boum,
Say the bells o' Canon Pyoum' (Pyon).

There is a fine old black-and-white dovecote, dated 1632, at Great Nupton, near by.

'Coffee and tea,
Say the bells of Weobley.'

If you want to see the devil in person go to Weobley church-yard at midnight, and walk slowly round the preaching cross seven times, saying the Lord's Prayer backwards, whereupon his Satanic Majesty will appear immediately. It is a pity that he did not appear to the architect who 'restored' the cross in the nineteenth century. Second thoughts, perhaps he did. Apart from a modern head, which is quite out of keeping with the old base, the niche for the pyx, or other sacred emblem, has been turned so that it now faces north instead of west. Here, and in other places, it was forgotten that if the worshipper is facing east the object of veneration should of necessity face west.

Of the town I cannot do better than quote from *Herefordshire*, edited by Arthur Mee. 'At every turn in this old town we come upon black and white houses with handsome gables, and it is one of the most picturesque streets in the whole county that leads us to the church. Its houses stand as if they had grown like flowers, along any line and to any height and shape they please, and their tiled roofs and gables and upper floors lean over the narrow pavements as if to whisper secrets to the passer-by.' The greater part of this description might well apply to many of the villages in Herefordshire: Pembridge, whose church has an isolated pagoda-like belfry, one of the finest of its kind; Eardisland, through which the Arrow glides, its banks exultant with the blossoms of cottage gardens; Kingsland, where there is a 'Volka' chapel on the east side of the north porch of the church. No one seems to know the meaning of the word Volka. The chapel is small, scarcely nine feet long and five feet wide, and has the floor raised as if for an altar. On the south side is an empty stone coffin, in which the skeleton of a woman and child were found. Perhaps the secret was buried in that coffin and another that may not be far away.

> 'Trip a trap a trencher,
> Say the bells of Lemster.'

Or alternatively:

> 'Up the cop and down the furrow,
> Say the bells of Leominster borough.'

This was the town that grew around the nunnery founded by Godiva, the wife of Leofric, Earl of Mercia and Lord of Coventry, and took its name from his, Leofminstre. Poor man, he achieved more fame by the story that he sent his wife out on that chilly ride than from all his lordships and earldoms. Whether he ever really did act in that ungallant way is, I think, doubtful. He wouldn't have been likely to behave like that in the early days of their marriage, and within three years of the ceremony he was endowing monasteries, so there wasn't very much time for him to be rough and tough. Hereford Cathedral still draws part of its income from manors which he presented to the see. But it would be a pity to rob the English-speaking world of such a source of thrills and blushes, so I will say no more than that the 'Peeping Tom' episode was added by a later chronicler, the earlier versions telling us that she passed through the market-place where the people were assembled, attended only by two soldiers, her long hair falling over her so that none could see her.

Isn't it an amazing state of affairs that whereas every other creature that isn't blind can look upon the opposite sex of its kind, in a natural state, whenever it desires, more or less; to man alone is such a thing so rarely possible that a story of this kind has been gloated over for nine hundred years? And it is the same all over the 'civilized' world. There are legends, in one form or another, from practically every country in Europe, telling of this perfectly natural curiosity in man and how, when detected, it has been punished in most unpleasant fashion. For example, on the island of Rügen, in the Baltic, on moonlight nights the goddess Hertha used at one time to come out of the forest to bathe in a lake. Any mortal who looked upon her was lured into the water and drowned. In the south there was poor Actaeon. Think of

what happened to him when, even by accident, he glimpsed Diana
at her bath.   Chewed up by his own hounds!

At St. Briavels, in the Forest of Dean, there is a legend that the
wife of the governor had, at one time, to ride naked round the
town once a year, and that King John, when he visited the district,
liked the idea so much that he ordered all the young maidens of
the town to do likewise.   St. Briavels, to-day, isn't what it was.
But, however lacking we may be in this country, there are islands
in the South Seas where such parades are held annually, and where
the marriageable maidens are as anxious to be admired as the
eligible bachelors are to admire.   There's a great deal to be said
for the custom, but, of course, the climate of England is against it.
I have, however, seen something of the kind in the old days in
Paris, where at the artists' dances there was usually a diversion
known as 'défilé des modèles.'   It was very charming.   Each
artist tried to get the prize for his favourite model, and we voted
by acclamation.

Of course these things can have a disturbing effect on a man
who is not used to them.   When Cuchulain, the demigod of
Ulster, came roaring into King Conchobar's camp, spoiling for a
fight and shouting murder, the women sought to distract his
thoughts by going out naked to meet him.   They succeeded.
When he saw thrice fifty of them approaching him, with eight
queens among them, all in that state, his blood boiled to such an
extent that they had to put him into a barrel of cold water to cool
him.   No sooner done than the water boiled in the barrel, so that
it burst the staves and the hoops 'like the cracking of nuts.'   The
result was hardly less when they put him into a second vat, for
then the water boiled with bubbles 'as big as a man's fists.'   It
wasn't until he had been through the process a third time that he
was in a fit state to sit quietly in the house and behave himself.
It is well known that he was a man of extremes.   Didn't he, while
still a boy, take on a hundred and fifty other boys all at the same
time, and lay them all out?   Didn't he bring to the ground eight
swans with one throw of a pebble from his sling, and sixteen more
of them with the next?   When he grew up he thought nothing
of killing a hundred men in an afternoon, slicing them down,
eight at a time, with blows of his sword.   He even defended
the whole of the Ulster frontier, single-handed, for months on

end, from the men of Connaught. It took a Munster man to kill him.

Even so, I can't help feeling that if I strayed over the Ulster border and saw eight queens and seven score and ten of their women coming to meet me, all stark naked, it might distract my thoughts from landscape painting.

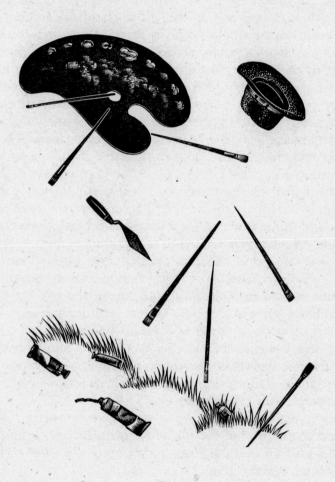

CHAPTER NINETEEN

LEOMINSTER, Pembridge, Weobley, Eardisland; all have exquisite churches dating from the twelfth, thirteenth, and fifteenth centuries. Kilpeck, on the other side of the river, has another, which, although one of the smallest in England, is one of our richest examples of Anglo-Norman Romanesque architecture.

Unfortunately, Victorian prudes defaced many of the quaint corbels that encircle the outside of the building, but that is nothing to what happened at Shobdon when, in 1753, the second Lord Bateman pulled down a church which was at least the equal of Kilpeck, and probably grander. He did this not only in order that he might indulge his taste in 'Strawberry Hill Gothic,' but also that he might have some ruins as features in his park, a form of absurdity then very fashionable. We read in one of Horace Walpole's letters of the same year to Richard Bentley: 'A little way from the town are the ruins of Lantony Priory: there remains a pretty old gateway, which G. Selwyn has begged, to erect on the top of his mountain, and it will have a charming effect.' Walpole himself was, of course, the arch-priest of this kind of vandalism, but the high-water mark of stupidity and insincerity was probably reached by 'one of the most notorious debauchees of the age,' who added a church spire to a country cottage in order that there should be a point of focus in the vista from his windows.

The noble Bateman has left us the present Shobdon church, which, though dedicated nominally to the Almighty, was more certainly intended for the greater glory of his lordship. It certainly helps to perpetuate his memory.

Entering by the west door we find ourselves in a setting of blue-and-white furniture, but the full refinement of the building is not disclosed until we reach a point higher up in the aisle. Then on our right we see the transept reserved for his lordship and his family, while on the left is the transept reserved for his lordship's servants. Both have their private doors leading into the church-yard, and both are railed off from the rest of the church, the one on the right having an extra screen of wood to keep out any possible draughts. It also has its own fire-place, and, whereas

the seats in the servants' apartment are no more than benches with
a narrow rail for the menial shoulder blades, there are thrones on
the other side of the aisle with sumptuous cushions for the noble
posteriors.   Special consideration was also shown to the vicar's
family, whose front seats, one on either side of the aisle, were
provided with doors.   My sympathy goes out to that family.
Don't I know well what it is to sit in the front seat of a church not
only under the eyes of one's own father, good and saintly as he
may be, but with the whole parish ranging away behind?   I'm
not sure that I didn't develop some mild form of phobia from
being stuck up there twice on every Sunday for twenty years.
No chance to get out, whatever pains afflicted me, without its
being an item in every parishioner's after-service conversation.
'Poor Masther Bob!   What happened to him?   'Twas in a
great hurry he was.'

I am surprised that his lordship allowed the fine old Norman
font to remain in the church, but perhaps he thought of it as 'a
feature,' as he certainly regarded the carved doors and tympana of
the old church when he re-erected them on the summit of a wind-
swept hill.   There, exposed to frost and rain, these carvings, in
soft stone designed for the interior of a building, have slowly
mouldered so that they are now but ghosts of their former glory.

But Herefordshire is noted for other things besides churches.
We read in Fuller's *Worthies of Herefordshire* that: 'This County
doth share as deep as any in the Alphabet of our English com-
modities, though exceeding in W, for Wood, Wheat, Wooll, and
Water.'   The author, referring to the first of these, says: 'This
Shire better answereth the name of *Pomerania*, then the Dukedome
of Germany so called, being a continued Orchard of Apple trees,
whereof much Sider is made.'   Of wheat we are told in Camden's
Britannia, 1607, that: 'So renowned also it is for Wheat, and bread
of the finest floure, that Lemster bread and Weabley Ale are
growne unto a common proverbe.'   Skelton, in one of his poems,
speaks of 'good Lemster woll,' and Drayton in *Poly-Olbion* refers
to the same as 'Lemster ore.'   The Ryeland breed of sheep is still
famous.   With such a river passing through it as the Wye that
'affords brumal Salmons, fat and sound,' there is no need to
wonder why water was included in the list of superlatives.

In more recent times two further Ws have been added—Wine
* D

and Women. The first of the two has already been mentioned under the name of Cyder, for that is undoubtedly the wine of the county, so much so indeed that in an old manuscript Bible preserved in Hereford Cathedral the scribe has written, in the fifteenth verse of the first chapter of St. Luke: 'He shal not drinke wyn ne cidir,' substituting, probably quite unconsciously, the name of the local beverage for the words 'strong drink' which occur in other versions.

Of women I am, of course, too diffident to speak, but I do re-member a very lovely creature who sat opposite to me in the train for over an hour, with her luggage labelled to Hereford. I will not give away my predilections by describing her, I will only say that her dress was as faultless as her features, and both of them displayed an 'exquisite reserve.' There was no question of con-versation between us because her father, a grumpy old man, was also in the carriage, but I 'll swear she read my thoughts, and I think I know what hers replied. Our eyes didn't even meet till she got up to leave the train, but then I caught a tiny flicker of an eyelid. I only mention this to show how perceptive as well as pictorially satisfying Herefordshire girls can be.

But even if there had been no others the county would have achieved fame with Mrs. Siddons and Elizabeth Barrett Browning. There was another girl too, one who, in her own words, 'was brought up in a brothel to fill strong water to the gentlemen'; one who, later became a king's mistress, 'the indiscreetest and wildest creature that ever was in Court.' In spite of this it was said that 'whatever she did became her,' and Dr. Thomas Tenison, after-wards Archbishop of Canterbury, when he preached her funeral sermon said 'much to her praise.' She certainly set an example to many of wider opportunity and narrower mind when among other bequests to charity she willed: 'That for showing my charity to those who differ from me in religion, I desire that fifty pounds may be put into the hands of Dr. Tenison and Mr. Warner, who, taking to them any two persons of the Roman Religion, may dis-pose of it for the use of the poor of that religion inhabiting the parish of St. James's aforesaid.' I refer, of course, to 'pretty, witty Nelly,' also known as Madam Eleanor Gwyn.

And now, with regret but no originality, to explode the myth about Dick Whittington. He wasn't born at Sollershope in

Herefordshire. It was at Pauntley in Gloucestershire that he first drew air into his lungs and squeaked the forerunners of stentorian aldermanic utterances. His father was Sir William Whittington, who died in 1360, and on his father's death Dick was apprenticed to Sir Ivo Fitzwarren, a Dorsetshire merchant of repute, whose daughter, in due course, he married. Nothing penniless and barefoot about that! These facts dispose of the legend that Dick, as a friendless boy, went to seek his fortune in London. The story of the cat is first found in the writings of a thirteenth-century Persian historian. How it came to the west is not known, but it was common in Europe before ever Whittington was born. It appears in Danish and Norwegian, in an Italian version, and in a Russian folk story, and in a Breton popular tale, the details being altered in each case to suit the nationality.

Even so, at Bryngwyn the ghost of a black cat is said to haunt the moat because Dick's daughter lived in the castle that once exercised dominion there.

CHAPTER TWENTY

I SAT IN THE GARDEN of the old chapter house at Hereford Cathedral one summer's morning wondering at the moaning and lamentation that was being offered up as worship. Butterflies flitted among the roses, bees snuffed at the lavender, a robin investigated the ripening seeds of a laburnum-tree—'golden chain' tree they call it down there. Two evacuee children wandered into the garden.

'Coo, look at them flowers. Say, mister, what d'you call them yeller flowers?' the elder girl asked me.

'They're roses,' I told her.

'Thought roses wus all pink; my name's Rose,' she said.

'And your sister?' I asked.

'Violet, 'er name's Violet. Any violets 'ere, mister?'

'None here,' I told her, 'but lots of them out in the fields. P'raps she's a wild violet?' I suggested.

'She's wild all right. Mind yerself on them stones: you'll break yer blinking neck,' she called to her sister who was clambering among the ruins. 'Wot's them big flowers, mister?'

'Hollyhocks,' I told her.

''Ollyocks?'

'That's right, 'ollyocks.'

Violet came over to join us.

'Look at them 'ollyocks, Violet, same colour your dress was.'

Our conversation was interrupted by an elderly lady and a younger companion who passed by.

'*Look* at that lavender,' said the younger of the two with enthusiasm.

'I want to show you the carvings in the Bishop's Cloister,' said the elderly one.

'It's heavenly,' sighed the younger, as she was led away.

Rose and Violet came back to me. 'See wot I got 'ere,' said Rose. 'A red beetle.'

'It's a ladybird,' I told her.

''Tisn't a bird,' she said scornfully, 'it's a beetle.'

Just then the ladybird opened its wings and flew away.

''E's right, it is a bird,' said Violet.

'It flies all the way from France,' I said.

'My dad was in France,' said Rose, 'but 'e didn't fly. 'E come back on a ship, says 'e vomited all the way. Didn't 'e, Vi?'

Two girls in W.A.A.F. uniform came in through the west door. 'Aren't they *lovely*?' said one. The other said nothing but bent down and smelled the blossoms.

A soldier and his girl came in and sat on the seat next to mine.

'Peaceful, isn't it?' she said.

He put his arm through hers.

'I love flowers,' she said.

'We'll have lots of 'em one day,' he answered.

'Lupins and delphiniums?' she asked.

'Stacks of 'em.'

A middle-aged man came and sat on the bench beside me. He was shabbily dressed and had a beard. I supposed that it was because I also had a beard that he spoke to me.

'Queer weather,' he said.

I agreed.

'For the time o' year you wouldn't think it was the time o' year.'

I agreed to that too.

He listened to some high-pitched intoning that floated through the window.

'If you want real religion to-day,' he said, 'you've got t' go to 'ospital.'

'They're kind in there?' I suggested.

'Kind! he said. 'Kind! Don't I know? Just bin there. Kind!'

'Where were you?' I asked.

'London. Westminster. Not far from 'Ouses o' Parliament. They got a big 'ospital there. A new one. 'Ad bombs on it too. They don't care. Took bad when staying with my brother-in-law. Ulcer in the stomach. They fixed me. Eat anything now. D'you know,' he said, suddenly lowering his voice, 'the disciples of Jesus say as how they saw Him walking on the water, but I seen the spirit o' God walkin' them wards at night. Movin' from bed to bed it was, bendin' over each one to see if 'e was asleep or no. What's more,' he added, his voice dropping almost to a whisper, 'when all the lights is put out, all but one little one on the floor, if you opens your eyes and looks up at the ceiling, you 'll see wings stretched out over your 'ead. Yes, big wings, from side to side o' the ward. 'E 's there all right.'

He got up, shook hands, and went out by the eastern gate. Before I went into the church I remembered how when I was in hospital in Lemnos in 1915, an Australian orderly sat by my bed all night holding my hand in his big horny fist while, in some form of delirium, my mind wandered ceaselessly through empty trenches, always returning to the same great empty dug-out. 'That 's all right, chum, I 've got you,' he used to say, whenever I opened my eyes. I can still feel the palm of his hand, rough as a file, but strong and kind.

Inside the church the remains of a bishop and a dean of the cathedral have been buried beside each other. Close friends, they died in the same year, 1691, and now the memorials which cover them are linked by clasped hands, and share the inscription *In vita conjuncti, in morte non divisi*. Near by, another memorial in the floor tells of less austere affections. Sir Richard Delabere, 1514, appears in brass with his two wives and twenty-one children. The other extreme of married life is portrayed on a stone in the north transept, where a knight and his lady are shown with a drawn dagger between them, and a cat and dog at their feet.

My emotions inside the great church were as mixed as the styles of architecture of which it is composed. If I was elated by the nobility of the Norman arches, and the serenity of the twelfth-century arcading in the south transept, I was depressed, as many another before me, by the restorations of the eighteenth century. If I was charmed by the graciousness and poetry of my guide, the verger, I was distressed that, in our own time, a memorial of blaring white marble should have been affixed to the mellow sandstone of one of the principal pillars of the nave.

In the evening I went back to the river. The water was dark, the trees lining the river were dark, while overhead a turmoil of slate-grey clouds blew across a western sky of ivory whiteness.

CHAPTER TWENTY-ONE

THE EULOGY OF VIRTUE in any one person may be palatable enough when administered in small doses, but when forcibly fed in large quantities it tends to disturb the mental digestion. History speaks fair of the Man of Ross, and he must certainly have been a good man, though perhaps a trifle dull. Perfection may be all right in heaven, but in this world it seems out of place. Purity of any kind can be carried too far. Even distilled water is mawkish.

You cannot get away from the virtues of this man in Ross or in any book that mentions Ross. You might think he was the only good man they had ever had in the town. Coleridge wrote poetry about him. Pope wrote poetry about him. Many rhymesters have written verse about him. But I'm not going even to write prose about him. The world isn't so scarce of good people as all that. I once asked an old man that I met in the County Kerry what his idea of happiness would be, and he answered: 'To be walking the roads of Ireland with a pocket full of money and to be dropping coins into every poor man's fist.' I once knew a woman of high degree whose daughter eloped, not before she had to. It wasn't the speck on the family name that worried this good mother: her chief anxiety was lest her daughter had been starving herself for the sake of her appearance before she left home.

It goes on all the time.

Wilton Castle, whose medieval ruins are on the west side of the sixteenth-century bridge, was once the seat of the de Greys, but the guide-book tells us that 'the first Lord Chandos obtained it by marrying Lord de Grey's sister.' It doesn't say if the price was considered high or low.

In 1580 Lord Arthur Grey became Lord Deputy of Ireland, and helped in the suppression of one of 'the troubles' that had arisen there. More important than that, he took Edmund Spenser to Ireland with him, and it was after the poet had settled down in a house of his own at Kilcolman in County Cork that he wrote much of *The Faerie Queene*. It was here, too, that he wrote his *Epithalamion* in honour of his bride, Elizabeth Boyle, a relative of Richard

Boyle, 'the great Earl of Cork,' whose favourite child was Robert Boyle of scientific fame.

Now it may interest few beyond myself that Spenser's property was almost neighbour to that which was to belong to some of my own antecedents about sixty years later. The first of my family to settle in Ireland, after trapesing over from Somersetshire, was a parson—we 've always been holy—who became rector of Kilcornan, near Limerick, about the year 1613. His three sons fought for Cromwell, and were granted acres and acres of land by the 'Protector,' who dispossessed the rightful owners and presented it, most generously, in lieu of pay, to my relations. I 'm glad to say it is no longer in the family.

It has been said that there are few places in the world, Herefordshire not excepted, where apples throve better than in that part of the country. The Toonmore pippin, which took its name from part of the estate, was celebrated for the quality of the cider it produced. So excellent, indeed, was the beverage produced from that apple that, on one occasion, the Royal Dublin Society withheld the prize which they had awarded to it on the ground that wine must have been added to the liquor. I wonder!

But it may be of more general interest that, in 1838, the daughter of a namesake of mine married no less a personage than Field Marshal Viscount Combermere, who amongst many other military exploits had been second in command to the Duke of Wellington at the battle of Salamanca. I have an idea that he remained second in command to my cousin Mary too, for whereas Wellington said of him that he was 'a fool and a damned fool, but the man to take Bhurtpore,' she was described by George Augustus Sala as 'a handsome lady with flashing eyes and very glossy black hair, very rich, very clever, and very witty: a brilliant musician, and a delightfully humorous artist.'

It is from her that we hear how a country vicar, wishing to please Wellington, who was paying a visit to his village, inquired of him if there was anything particular he would like the Sunday sermon to be about. 'About ten minutes,' replied the duke.

Soon after their marriage Combermere was appointed Governor of Barbados, and it was during his tenure of office that strange happenings in one of the graveyards on that island reached their culmination. This again we hear of from his wife's pen.

The burial-ground adjacent to Christ Church, Barbados, is on a shelf of coral, a hundred feet above sea level, and the floors of the vaults were sunk deep into this coral. The vault with which our story is concerned belonged to the family of the Hon. Colonel Chase. Its walls, its roof, and its floor were of stone and cement throughout. The door was a single solid slab of stone, sealed with cement.

On 9th August 1812, when the tomb had been opened for an interment, it was found that two of the coffins had been moved from their places. One of them, a large leaden one, lay on the ground; another, that of a child, had been thrown from one side of the tomb to the opposite corner. The church officials, therefore, made a careful inspection to see if there could be any way of entrance other than by the door. Finding none, they rearranged the coffins and sealed the tomb. Four years and two months later the vault had to be opened for another interment, but, though the door was exactly as it had been left, and the cement as hard as stone, the confusion inside was even greater than before. The same thing happened again, twice.

Lord Combermere then decided to investigate the matter in person. With members of his staff he visited the vault, and 'in his presence every part of the floor was sounded to ascertain that no subterranean passage or entrance was concealed. It was found to be perfectly firm and solid; no crack was even apparent . . . the three sides, together with the roof and flooring, presented a structure as solid as if formed of entire slabs of stone.' After the mourners had retired the floor was carefully sprinkled with fine white sand in the presence of Lord Combermere and the assembled crowd, and when the masons had sealed the door Lord Combermere made several impressions in the cement with his own private seal. Many of those attending added their private marks.

The interest in these events increased, so much so that, nine months after the last interment, Lord Combermere consented to have the tomb reopened, and was again present at the ceremony. He found the cement on the door unbroken and the impressions of his seal as perfect as when they were made. Those who had added private marks found those marks intact. Having broken the cement the masons attempted to move the great stone, but it was only with the greatest difficulty that they were able to move it sufficiently for a man to enter the tomb. Then it was found that a large leaden coffin was leaning almost vertically against the inside of the stone door, and although normally it would have required seven or eight men to move it, there was no trace of footprints on the sanded floor. In addition to this, a child's coffin had been hurled against one of the walls with such force that a deep scar had been made in the stonework.

The Chase family, therefore, ordered the coffins to be removed and buried in separate graves; after which the vault was abandoned and has never since been used. As far as I am aware there has been no satisfactory explanation of these occurrences.

If, on our journey back from the West Indies, we had overstepped our mark at Ross by about ten miles we should have found ourselves at Speech House in the Forest of Dean. This is not only the legal but the geographical centre of that hilly wooded triangle of some twenty thousand acres which lies to the east of the Wye below Ross. In *The Laws of the Dean Forest* we are told that: 'A Forest, in contemplation of law, is a certain territory of woody grounds and fruitful pastures, privileged for wild beasts and fowls of forest, chase and warren to rest and abide there in the safe protection of the king for his delight and pleasure . . . and replenished with wild beasts of venery and chase, and with great coverts of vert for the succour of the said beasts there to abide.' It is added that: 'The beasts of the forest are the hart, the hind, the buck and the doe, and the hare, the wild boar, the wolf, the fox and the marten, all male as well as female. . . . All beasts of the forest which are fit for food, but none other, are in law venison.'

Few of these beasts are to be found there to-day; neither are there many of those birds that men delight to shoot. But the jay, as resplendent as he is garrulous, is to be seen on all sides. ''Andsomest birds in the forest,' I was told. 'Thrippence 'a'penny a pair of legs we get for 'em. Some sells the wings as well, for fly-fishers.' Tree creepers are there, too, in quantity, but they are unmolested. They seemed to be on every other oak. Redstarts flirting their wings and tail were like small spurts of flame in the sunlight. One of them, a cock, perched close to where I was sitting. As he faced me his white forehead and black throat were framed by the gold of his quivering tail and wings. Suddenly he disappeared into a hole in a dead tree. But it was only a moment before he was out again. Then he flew away. Almost immediately the hen arrived and, without wasting time, went into the same hole, remaining there for half an hour. After she had gone I peered inside, and could just make out two pale-blue eggs, some eighteen inches down, in the cavity.

The timber of the forest has always been famous, particularly the oaks for ship-building, so much so that, as John Evelyn tells us in his *Sylva*, 'in the great expedition of 1588 it was expressly enjoined the Spanish Commanders of that signal Armada that if, when landed, they should not be able to subdue our nation and make good their conquest, they should yet be sure not to leave a tree standing in the Forest of Dean.' To-day the oldest and largest holly trees in the British Isles are to be seen in Speech House wood. And if the oaks are tough and strong so also are the men who live among them, the foresters. Strong in body, strong in will, 'a robustic wild people,' they live unto themselves, abiding by their own laws.

Speech House, now a hotel, and a very delightful one too, has been the court house of the forest since the time of Charles II, and the court of verderers, instituted in 1016 by King Canute, to make and maintain the laws of the forest, still meets there. At one time this court held power of life and death, and it seems to have had no particular qualms about using that power when transgressors were brought before it. Many of these laws are unique, and the foresters are jealous of their privileges. To quote but one example, coal mines are only leased to free miners, that is to say men who, born in the hundred of St. Briavels, have worked in one of the forest mines for a year and a day. A grant to a free miner is called a gale: the principal officer of the forest, whose duty it is to grant the gales, is called the gaveller.

The coal seams being, for the most part, at no great distance from the surface of the ground, quite primitive methods of working them still obtain good results. It is only a few years since a father used to lower his son down the shaft in a bucket by means of a windlass, using the same contrivance to bring the coal, dug by his son, to the surface.

The iron mines date back to the time of the Romans who not only exploited the mineral wealth of the forest, but traversed the district with roads, the remains of which are in many places still in evidence. Much of the imperfectly smelted ore of that period has since been worked at a profit. Good building stone, too, is quarried in the forest, and red ochre is obtained in quantity from pits near Coleford. Many of the mines have names which seem significant. 'Standfast Old Level' suggests a steady if not spectacular flow of coal. 'Work or Hang' implies more stubborn seams. 'Strip-and-at-it' must surely promise reward for honest labour. 'As you like it' hints at easy money. Contrary to what one might expect, these mines dotted about the forest are for the most part unobtrusive, and do little to spoil the grandeur and pageantry of the scene.

Camping in the forest is strictly forbidden, as I read on a notice which I found within a few yards of where I had spent a very pleasant night. Although the sunset of the evening before had been brilliant, and, looking to the west, the heart of the forest had been like the heart of a fire, the morning broke grey and misty with spiders' gossamer, dew-laden, on every bracken frond, and the silken threads of caterpillars sparkling from every oak. The birds seemed loath to sing and, as I walked along the close-cropped dewy grass paths, the dominating sounds were the tapping of woodpeckers and the raucous cries of jays.

It was in May, and the spruces were tasselled with young green. The firs were putting out their crimson shoots. The beeches told bright against the sombre evergreens and oaks. The young bracken was unfolding its crosier-like stalks. Nebulae of stitch-wort starred a firmament of bluebells.

By midday the sun had broken through. Bees were in the foxgloves and about the holly-trees. A queen wasp in her black-and-yellow livery hovered over the green lichen on a dead tree.

'Never stand up agin the Almighty,' said a forester, when he saw me looking at a tree that had been struck by lightning. 'That oak 'eld up 'is 'ead above the others, and see now, split from 'ead to foot, all the sixty foot of 'im. Matchwood,' he said, handing me a bundle of fibres which, indeed, were no thicker than matches. The general theory for this effect of lightning is that the moisture in the tree being suddenly converted into steam by the heat, the extra pressure bursts the fibres apart.

Later in the day I was in 'the local' when a big rough-looking man came in. He had with him a young sheep-dog bitch.

'Sit down,' he said to the dog, almost in a whisper.

The dog obeyed.   Then its owner ordered a pint of beer and a packet of biscuits.   He looked me up and down, but said nothing while being served.

'A pretty pup,' I ventured.

He looked at me again, dipped one of his biscuits in the beer, and gave it to the dog.

''Er parents won up in Scotland,' he said.   ''Er and me shares.' Then he ate a biscuit.

''Er and me shares,' he repeated.   'Don't we?' he said, looking at the dog.

The dog put her two front feet on his knee.

'Sit down,' he said quietly.

She did so.

'Very tender,' he said, 'bit eager; won't work with no other dog.   She 'll come lovely.'

Again the dog put her feet on his knee.

'Sit down,' he said, as quietly as before.

The dog obeyed.

'Very tender, got to take her gentle like.'   He gave her another biscuit and took one himself.   'She 'll come lovely,' he said, as he watched her eating.   He dipped the last biscuit in the beer, and gave it to her.   Then he swallowed what remained of his pint and went out.

CHAPTER TWENTY-TWO

THE MAIN ROAD from Mitcheldean station to Ross runs through a valley that was once a course of the Wye. In those days the river wound its way to the north of where Ross now stands, circling Penyard hill and Purland woods before it took its present course from about a mile below the town. This was one of those big meanders which in the course of some ten million years have been short-circuited by the eroding action of the river itself. Another occurs at Redbrook, and a third at Bigsweir. Dr. Austin Miller, who had made a scientific study of the subject, is of opinion that several of the loops still existing, such as those at Symond's Yat, Tintern, and Lancaut, will also be superseded, and that at some long-distant date the Wye will run an even shorter course to the sea.

At first sight it seems odd that the river flowing quietly over the plain at Ross should suddenly cut its way into the hills below Goodrich, and continue a tortuous course for some miles before emerging into the open at Symond's Yat. Still more odd, it seems, that having found again the rich alluvial valley, with little to impede its progress, it should almost immediately charge back and batter itself among the rocks and cliffs of the Forest of Dean. A similar vagary occurs round about Monmouth. Roman road-builders, Norman road-builders, modern railway engineers have all chosen the easier route. Why did the river behave differently? As with the lawns at Oxford it is only a matter of time. Many millions of years ago, before the present lowlands were worn down, the river bed was six hundred feet above its present level. The stream chose what was then the easiest way.

I had hoped to find a boat at Hay, a boat that would carry me, at leisure and in comfort, to the sea. But at Hay they referred me to Hereford, and at Hereford they suggested Ross. At Ross they were unable to help. The fact is that on the Wye the only idea connected with a boat is that it should be hired by the hour and brought back before dark. In my extremity I paid a hurried visit to London in the hope of buying a canoe. If the stout lady who was turning over the pages of *Sweet Thames* in the book department

of the Army and Navy Stores had realized that the stout gentleman who was writhing on the floor of the next department,
trying to extricate himself from the embraces of a collapsible canoe,

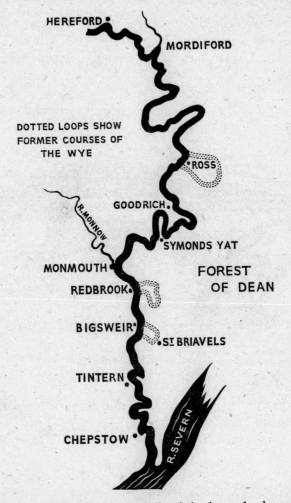

was the author of that same book I might have had another copy
to autograph. My visit was fruitless. I got some new studs put
in the soles of my shoes and went back to the roads.

A few miles below Ross I inquired of three men in Home Guard
uniform how I might best find my way to Goodrich. At first
they were not communicative. They seemed, in fact, a little
suspicious. But when I showed them my own Home Guard

enrolment card their manner changed. They were waiting for a bus which was to take them to their headquarters for a field-day. One of them was a farmer, another was an ex-jockey, the third had been a soldier.

'If I was to tell you the trouble I 've 'ad this year with phlebitis in me legs and wireworms in me farm you wouldn't believe it. Shocking, I tell you. Never did see such wireworms, and as to my legs——'

'You wouldn 't 'a ' done in the Khyber Pass,' interrupted the soldier; ''ad to be fit out there to dodge the boulders the niggers rolled down on you'.

'One scratch on my legs and they don't heal for a six month,' continued the farmer.

'I wish they 'd give us 'orses,' said the jockey. 'I reckon a 'orse worth six cars across country.'

'Civvy 'orses no good under fire,' said the soldier. 'Not trained to it.'

'We ain't got ter stand under fire,' replied the jockey. 'We got ter nip along and hinform.'

'I wonder how many of us could hit a parachutist?' I ventured.

'No 'arder than a peacock,' said the soldier. 'Ever shot pea-cocks, sir? Fine sport that. I shot twenty of 'em before breakfast in the jungle. They 's fine eating all right too.'

Before I could hear further murderous details the khaki-laden coach appeared, and I was left to continue my way.

Goodrich Court, in fourteenth-century style, was built in the nineteenth century. Goodrich Castle, a genuine antique and a noble one, dates from Norman times. Thanks to the Office of Works it is in a fine state of preservation. It is said that at one time in its history earth was brought from Ireland to floor the cellars, so that no toad could live there. If that is true it was done in great ignorance, and it can only have led to disappointment all round, for the holy Patrick, though exceedingly strict with the serpents, made no objection at all to a few of these tailless batrachians remaining in the west.

But another connection between Goodrich and Ireland is more historical. The Rev. Thomas Swift, once vicar of the parish, was grandfather of the Dean of St. Patrick's. If ever an apple brought trouble to a man, since Eden, it was to this poor parson. The only son of his mother, and she an heiress, he was disinherited by her merely because, while still a boy, he had robbed an orchard. In spite of that he brought up fourteen children, one of whom became father of Jonathan Swift, Dean of St. Patrick's. The Rev. Thomas, was a great Royalist, even to the extent of mortgaging his small estate so that he could convey 'three hundred broad pieces' to Charles I when he was in difficulties after Naseby. 'I am come,' said he, to the governor of Raglan Castle, where Charles was resting, 'to give His Majesty my coat.' The governor hinted delicately that the garment wasn't of much value. 'Why then, take my waistcoat,' said Swift, suiting the action to the word. In the lining he had quilted the whole three hundred gold pieces, and it was remarked by one of those near to Charles that 'the King had received no supply more seasonable or acceptable than these three hundred broad pieces during the whole war, his distress being then very great and his resources cut off.'

Swift suffered in more ways than one for his loyalty. He was 'ejected from his preferments,' and his wife was 'most inhumanely dealt with by a stony-hearted rebel.' But, though deprived of his living, he remained in the neighbourhood. To assist him in his private ministration he caused a special chalice to be made. This afterwards came into the possession of his grandson, who presented it to Goodrich church with an inscription carved upon it, in Latin, of which the following is a translation:

'Thomas Swift, Vicar of this Church, well known in History for what he did and suffered for the late Charles, administered out

of this same Chalice to the sick.   Jonathan Swift, S.T.D., Dean
of the Church of Saint Patrick, Dublin, grandson of the aforesaid
Thomas, dedicates this Cup to this Church for ever.   1726.'

The dean, as may be remembered, when travelling between
England and Ireland, often made the journey from London to
Holyhead on foot.   In the course of one of these peregrinations
he had occasion to put up at a village in Shropshire, not far from
the Welsh border.   While there he attended divine service, and
was not a little surprised to hear the preacher declaim with great
emphasis a sermon of the dean's own composition.   Compli-
menting the preacher afterwards, he observed that the sermon he
had just heard had cost him months of thought, but he could never
have hoped to give it such a delivery.   'Indeed,' he added,
'you have such a power of oratory that I declare you have
done more honour to my sermon this day that I could myself,'
whereupon he pressed half a guinea into the affrighted preacher's
hand.

It was in the courtyard of Goodrich Castle that Wordsworth
met the simple child that lightly drew its breath, but of the resultant
poem the less said the better.   I would rather refer to a more
robust ballad connected with Courtfield, two miles further downstream.   This estate was once known as Greenfield, but after
King Henry V, as a sickly infant, had been nurtured there it
became known by its present name.   The property at one time
belonged to the Vaughan family, who trace their ancestry back
to Sir Cradoc, a Knight of the Round Table; and it was Sir Cradoc's
wife, a daughter of King Palinor, Prince of South Wales, who was
the heroine of the ballad.   In it a boy is made to enter the court
of King Arthur carrying with him a magic mantle.   This mantle
was such that only a woman of the strictest virtue could wear it,
and the ballad tells how each of the ladies of the court was, in
turn, challenged by her husband to wear the garment, and of the
disasters that followed.   Naturally the queen was given precedence
in the ceremony, but:

'When she had taen the mantle,
     And all was with it cladde,
From top to toe it shiver'd down
     As tho' with sheers beshradde.

'One while it was too long
　　Another while too short,
And wrinkled on her shoulders
　　In most unseemly sort.'

After the queen, 'Sir Kay call'd forth his lady.'

'When she had taen the mantle,
　　With purpose for to wear:
It shrunk up to her shoulder,
　　And left her backside bare.'

Most embarrassing. Similar unfortunate results occurred to
others, until it came to Sir Cradoc's turn.

'Sir Cradock call'd his lady,
　　And bade her to come neare.
Come win this mantle, lady,
　　And do me credit here.'

This time the tell-tale garment did little more than wrinkle about
the hem. Even so, it was enough to alarm the lady. She begged
a moment's respite. Just one moment and she would confess
everything. Hurriedly she told:

'Once I kist Sir Cradocke
　　Beneathe the green wood tree:
Once I kist Sir Cradocke's mouth
　　Before he married mee.'

Charming!

Symond's Yat is, of course, the beauty spot on the river. You
struggle up a hill so steep that people coming down suggest that
it is easier going up. You don't agree with them. Just before
you reach the summit you can, if you wish, stop at a tin hut and
buy embroidered pillow-covers, flower vases, jig-saw puzzles, and
Union Jacks. From there it is only a hundred yards to the rock
whence the great panorama is unfolded.

'Cor, blimey! Look at this, 'Erb.'

'Ruddy 'igh, ain't it?' says 'Erb.

Far below, on either side, the river flows north, flows south.
To the east Coppet Hill, bare, smooth and streamlined; to the west
the richly wooded slopes of Great Doward. There are plenty of

houses on this western hill, and few of them improve the land-scape, but they have 'roses round the doors,' geraniums, phloxes, and sweet williams in the gardens, and nasturtiums on the trellises.

It always surprises me that those who take a house in the country or by the sea for a month in the summer should be so scornful of those who only take rooms for a week, while those in rooms feel

superior to the day visitors. The day visitors in their turn look askance at the conducted parties. We are all of us trippers in this world. Don't let us be intolerant of the music from the char-à-banc that is behind us. It is possible that our own noise may be equally trying to those who are travelling ahead.

In the great gorge that leads to Monmouth tall towers of lime-stone stand out from the richly wooded slopes. Trees smother the cliffs and festoons of wild clematis smother the trees. Branches spread over the water, and in their shadows moorhens hide. A cormorant flies heavily upstream. A salmon splashes. A fisher-man sits for hours on the bank beside a home-made rod and line.

'Eels,' he said, 'takes a bit o' patience.' The river winds, and winds again. Here a silver pool reflecting the tansy, meadow-sweet, and toadflax on the bank, there a beer-brown scour with purple lights below each hidden rock.

'Have you seen a dead rabbit anywhere?' asked a small boy who was wandering in the woods with a butterfly net.

'I have not,' I said, 'but there was a very live weasel playing hide-and-seek with me a few yards back. If you follow him you might get one.'

'I want a rotten one,' he said.

'Sorry I can't oblige. What do you want it for? Flies for fishing, I suppose, or maggots?'

'Butterflies,' he answered. Then in a subdued voice as if confiding a great secret he added: 'Purple Emperors.'

'I thought butterflies liked flowers.'

'Not emperors. Dad says: "Rotten Rabbits for Purple Emperors."'

At one moment the boy's eyes were searching the undergrowth for some putrescent corpse, the next he was staring up among the oak branches watching for the fluttering of one of our loveliest and rarest butterflies. I left him to his search, wondering as I went along at the queer tastes of emperors. When I reached a sheltered path through the wood and found it reeking with strong tobacco smoke I wondered at the queer tastes of commoners.

The smoke came from a middle-aged man who was leaning over a stile near the edge of the wood. His foot was bound up. He had had some sort of an accident with the wheel of a wagon. 'I'll be younger when I'm older,' he told me.

And so to Monmouth, where relics of Nelson bedazzle the visitor, and the Monnow, tumbling from the Black Mountains, flows under the medieval fortified toll-bridge.

On the day that I was there the talk of the town concerned a thirty-one-pound pike which, in perfect condition, had been caught that morning in the river. The fisherman was an expert. He knew that in that particular pool the fish would make a rush through some tangled debris and so break his line. He didn't give it a chance. Holding the rod taut with his left hand, as the fish dashed past him he struck with the gaff, with his right, and thus within three minutes of being hooked it was on the bank and its hunting days ended for ever.

Among fish, relatively, the pike has one of the smallest of brains, and though, as in humans, that need not imply a lack of physical attraction, it cannot be said that the fish has an endearing expression, however impartial one's attitude. It is that great shelf of upturned bradawls, acting as a lower jaw, surmounted by an eye that lacks anything of the innocence of salmon, trout, or perch, which renders the creature so repellent. And its features and expression are an indication of its character. The pike has a gluttonous soul. J. R. Norman in his *History of Fishes* says: 'The Pike is almost unsurpassed in greediness and ferocity, and when on the feed nothing comes amiss to its insatiable maw.' Even members of its own species are not immune. H. Cholmondeley-Pennell, an inspector of fisheries, has put on record the following instance which came directly within his own experience. A night line had been set in the Avon, and when taken up next morning was found to have a large pike on the hook. In order to extract the hook this fish had to be opened, and it was then found that the hook was really inside a smaller fish, which had been swallowed by the bigger one. This smaller one was then opened, and it was found that yet another pike was inside its belly. It wasn't until this third fish of about three-quarters of a pound had been opened that the hook was extricated. The same writer mentions that he had himself, on several occasions, taken pike with others in their stomachs.

It has been estimated that a pike will consume in a single day its own weight of food, so great is its appetite and so rapid its digestion. In addition to the armament on the lower jaw the palate of the fish bristles with small incurved teeth which, being attached to flexible plates, can be depressed to admit the victim, and then raised to prevent its escape. My curiosity as to their sharpness was satisfied, with emphasis, when having touched these teeth lightly I found my fingers bleeding profusely.

While the record specimen for rivers of the British Isles was caught in the Wye, many of far greater dimensions have been taken from lochs and meres. The largest 'by fair angling,' fifty-three pounds, was caught in Lough Conn in County Mayo, but the skeleton of a head from Loch Ken in Kirkcudbrightshire is still preserved, and suggests that the reputed weight of its owner, seventy-two pounds, is, probably, not greatly exaggerated. A monster, nineteen feet in length, and weighing five hundred and fifty pounds, was *said* to have been captured in a lake in Württemberg in 1497, but when, in the course of years, its backbone was examined by a zoologist, it was found that the number of its vertebrae far exceeded the usual ration supplied by nature. In other words, like dried mermaids supplied by the Chinese, it was a fake.

CHAPTER TWENTY-THREE

IT WAS EVENING when I stepped ashore by the old Anchor Inn at Tintern, the evening of the harvest moon. On that night, in less prosaic times, lovers came from far and near to whisper promises to each other while, from the west end of the abbey, they watched the full moon fill the great empty circle in the head of the eastern window.

The building was glowing in the evening light, warm as the rose-tinted walls of Petra. After sunset a shimmering veil of mist filled the valley, through which the church appeared tenuous and unsubstantial.

I wandered among the idle pillars and arches while the evening lost its light. Dew began to fall. Owls called from wood to wood 'Oo, ooloo oo. Oo, ooloo oo.' It grew darker. A pig grunted; a calf bellowed. Still darker. A woman and a man palavered on the road. Dark cars rushed past in the darkness. 'Oo, ooloo ooloo oo.'

Then over the high, wooded, eastern hill came the moon, golden in the deep indigo sky. Steadily it grew from a shallow crescent to a fuller arc, then to a half circle, to three-quarters, to the full sphere of light. I was alone, and had no wish for whispers from any one. From the southern meadow I watched the shadows creep into the aisles, and the transepts emerge from dark shapes of their own creating.

As the mist cleared away the church stood revealed in the moonlight, so calm, so still, yet no calmer than the bones of those who lie beneath its turf; priests, deacons, laymen, all who, in their own way, have swelled the universal song of praise. Some of us worship life because we fear death, some of us worship death because we fear life. There is room for us all. Jackdaws now praise God where once the white-robed monks sang hymns.

After the grand orchestra of the hills through which the Wye finds its course Tintern may seem but the reed-song of a boy, yet no chord of praise was ever better tuned. The ruin is so perfect now that it is difficult to believe it could ever have been nobler. I, for one, could not wish one more stone upon another.

When I think of those empty traceries, framing vistas of wooded hills and valley, I am reminded of a little church in the far south of Ireland, where every window but one is of painted glass.

Through that single exception there may be seen as fair a view as any in this world, a lough of deepest blue, studded with green islets, and backed by range after range of purple hills. Under the window is the inscription: 'The heavens declare the glory of God, and the firmament showeth his handiwork.'

At Tintern the river becomes tidal. To quote Tennyson's well-known lines:

E

'There twice a day . . .
The salt sea-water passes by,
And hushes half the babbling Wye,
And makes a silence in the hills.'

The weather had been changeable, cold one moment and hot
the next. Heavy showers seemed to descend from nowhere. If
the glass was high, it rained; if the glass was low, the days were
fine. 'Queer weather,' I observed to a man who was clearing
the gutters on the Chepstow road. 'Queer weather?' he repeated,
'I should say it was. We gets queer weather here, queer weather
all over Wales. You should 'a' been here in 1933, in September
'33, thunder and lightnin', the lightnin' first, mind you, and 'ail-
stones big as walnuts. Some says they wur big as eggs, but they
wusn't. Nine foot deep on the road they wur, couldn't get along the
road to St. Arvans. We thought as it was the end of the world.'

It wasn't quite as bad as that in 1941. Even so, that same
evening when I got into the 'George' at Chepstow I was cold
and wet. I only wanted a drink, some food, a bath, and a bed.
While dealing with the first—and most essential—I heard a voice
behind me: 'Got a ha'penny on you? You don't remember
me?' added the speaker, when I turned to face him.

'I do,' I said, 'but not where we met.'

'I promised you a knife, one that would keep its edge. I've
been carrying it for you for months.' He dropped a penknife
into my pocket.

'You 're Arthur Harris,' I said, 'and we met at Llangurig, and
we talked about steel. But you never promised me a knife.'

'I did,' he said. 'It 's yours.'

I handed over the halfpenny.

'What are you doing here?' I asked.

'Cars.'

'How long are you staying?'

'To-morrow. Going back in the morning. Want a lift?'

'Can't,' I said. 'Got to explore the town.'

'You 're under suspicion.'

'Me?'

'What were you doing at Beachley Head this afternoon?'

'Looking for dunlin on the mud.'

'There was some as thought different,' laughed a man in coast-guard uniform. 'If you 'd 'a ' put them glasses up, you was for it.'

'You were for it, any way,' said Harris, 'if I hadn't told them who you were.'

'I want to find out about the elvers,' I said.

'Elvers?'

'Didn't you know there was an elver industry here, used to ship tons of them to Germany every year before the war?'

'If you wants to see elvers,' said the coastguard, 'cut three inches off the ends of a hay-fork. Then you 've got 'em proper.'

'There 's a lot of salmon netting at the mouth of the river. Stopping nets, lave nets, tuck nets. I want to see something of them.'

'You 'll be tucked up in a police net yourself if you 're not careful.'

'I 've got to inquire about coracles.'

'Haven't been used since 1914.'

'You 'd better come back with me,' said Harris.

'There 's the castle to be seen.'

'What about it?'

'Full of history: Marten the regicide, Jeremy Taylor.'

'Plenty of history in Wales.'

The door opened and a man came in in oilskin and sou'wester.

'Raining?'

'Teeming, settled in for a week.'

'Noon to-morrow we 'll start?' said Harris.

For a moment I hesitated. Then I agreed, and as I did so I felt my spirits rise.

CHAPTER TWENTY-FOUR

AND SO, with the rain still pouring, we raced along the road that follows the Wye almost the whole way from its mouth to its source. We passed Whitebrook, where the stream ran white from the limestone; we passed Redbrook, where the stream ran red from the sandstone. We went through Monmouth, and thence over the hills to Hereford, passing Wormelow Tump, thought, by some, to be where Arthur fought his last battle, with Mordred.

While we were having lunch under the fifteenth-century cusped timbers of the dining-room in the Booth Hall Hotel at Hereford, Harris pushed a fountain pen across the table. 'That's yours,' he told me. 'I promised it to you.'

'You didn't,' I said, 'and I don't believe that other yarn about the knife either.'

'Try the nib,' he suggested.

I did so. It was the best I'd known since my favourite pen was pinched in Barcelona.

'It's yours,' he said. 'Put it in your pocket.'

There was no arguing with the man. He can't help it. He is always giving things away. He makes a hobby of it.

He had business to do in the town, so we didn't get away till after three o'clock. Meanwhile I had time to drop in and see my friend, Mr. F. C. Morgan, at the museum. It was through his help that I had visited many of the churches of Herefordshire on my way down. Harris called for me at four o'clock.

At Bredwardine we crossed what is said to be one of the finest brick bridges in England—even so, not impressive—and when the sun broke through the clouds we stopped to visit the cow-pond, near Winforton, where, in 1923, Miss Doreen Davey caught the record salmon, weighing fifty-nine pounds. Hooked late in the evening, it was almost two hours before, by the light of a bonfire, its fight for life was ended, 'one hour and fifty-five minutes of concentrated excitement and real hard work,' on the part of the lady.

On to Hay, and past Erwood Inn, where Henry Mayhew, hiding from his creditors, conceived the idea of *Punch*, our national monument. 'Never read the book meself, but I'm told it's a good one,' said an inhabitant. Through Builth, and over the Ithon at Newbridge; good spawning grounds in that stream. The further we got into the mountains the more my spirits rose. In the evening light the sky was red as apples and the river was lichen-green. A rising fish left an inky stain on the water.

Into Rhayader. There's Robert Riddell and Richard Ashton by the war memorial. What's that yarn Riddell is telling? 'It was seeing you coming along that reminded me of it,' he said. 'There were two bearded brothers, one a poacher and the other a preacher. When the poacher was caught one Sunday he gave his brother's name. Then he went home and shaved. When the summons came along it was in the preacher's name. Of course he had his whole congregation to prove an alibi. The bailiff was new to the district. He's still looking for the offender.'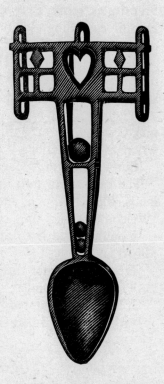

'I want you a moment,' called Gordon Lewis to me from the door of the 'Castle.' 'Have a look at this,' he said, taking an elaborately carved wooden spoon from the wall of the bar. 'A love spoon,' he said. 'They used to be given instead of engagement rings. A boy would spend most of a winter's evenings carving one of them for the girl he'd set his mind on. If she accepted it, 'twas the same as a promise of marriage. Those beads in the stem showed the number of children he would like to have. Apple wood, I believe they were made from. The tree of love! Some of them were much more elaborate; might be two spoons joined together by a chain, all carved from one piece of wood. The more elaborate they were, the more they showed a man's skill and constancy. The custom has died out this last century. Some say it's the origin of the word spooning. I picked that one up for a few pence at a jumble sale.'

'Leave your wooden spoons,' said Arthur Harris. 'I 'm in love with Llangurig.'

'Ten miles to go,' I said, getting into the car beside him.

On we went, under the great Gamallt hump, and over the Marteg, a wonderful stream for trout. A fisherman told me that, once, he 'd caught a hundred fish there in less than two hours. Five miles more, four miles. There 's the foot-bridge, and the Dernol cascading down from Carn-y-Groes. Three miles, two miles. Was that Kinsey Morgan going back to Rhayader?

One mile, Clochfaen Hall on the other side of the river. They once had a hirlas, or drinking-horn, there; fifteen inches long, silver-mounted, and held three-quarters of a pint.

'There 's Gwilym! And there 's Maggie and Gwyneth. Lovely girl, Gwyneth; you 'd think she and her mother were sisters. *Mind* where you 're driving!'

'Sorry,' he said. 'I was thinking of Gwyneth.'

The car swung into the yard of the 'Black Lion.' Jack Rowlands, Bill Rhosgoch, and Edgar Blaenglyn came out to meet me. 'Welcome home,' they said.

'Your cottage is to let,' said Dick Hughes the postman, who joined us.

'It 's in the paper this week,' said Jack.

'The roof is mended,' said Bill.

'It 's all been painted,' said Edgar.

Within a week I had signed a tenant's agreement.

CHAPTER TWENTY-FIVE

IT WAS NOT UNTIL the first week in December that I was able to go into residence. It was the sixth day of the month, to be exact, and surely the wettest day of the year.

'Are you going?' asked Dai, that morning as we looked out of the window of the 'Black Lion' at the deluge that blotted out the valley.

'You 'll be drowned,' said Tom Owen.

'You 'll be bogged,' said Ivor Morgan.

'I 'm going with Trevor Jones,' I said, 'as soon as he brings his car back from the funeral.'

'We 'll be walking after you in a few days if you 're not careful,' said Bill Rhosgoch.

'He 'll be a tidy weight to lift,' said the village carpenter.

'Lift your glasses now,' I said, and with that we sat down around the fire and waited for the taxi.

It wasn't a case of 'Would the car get there?' but of 'How far would it get?' 'Yes, yes, it would go the first mile all right: wasn't the road metalled? But what would happen after that? How would we travel on the green track to Tyn-y-bryn? There was bound to be a fountain down the road from Coedcochion. 'Twas a steep climb surely. Five hundred feet, they say, from bottom to top. Would the car ever take them corners? Would his tyres grip? Were his brakes good? Wouldn't it be better to go round and over the back of the hill? No, the road was sunk in the bog up there.'

As things happened the most pessimistic among them turned out to have been optimistic. We didn't get five hundred yards up the green track before the car was axle-deep in the mud, with the two back tyres revolving as if they were fly-wheels. When we got out of the car we sank up to our ankles. We collected sticks and stones, and laid them before the tyres as enticingly as if they had been saucers of milk before sick kittens. They might have been bread and milk for all the effect they had on the tyres. Then the engine boiled. Trevor said there was a leak in the engine. The radiator must have been the only thing in Montgomeryshire that day that was short of water.

'Cobbler should be about,' said Trevor, 'he said he'd be on the look-out.'

'Will I try him with a shout?' I asked.

'You might,' he said.

With that I let out a bellow that might have been the mating call of a bull, the way it echoed across the valley.

'Hallo,' said Cobbler, coming out of a cattle-shed near by.

There was no need to describe the situation to him. It was plain enough, and he had foreseen it. Away he went up the hill at a trot, and within ten minutes he was back again, accompanied by Jack Brown and his carter Richey Evans, who brought with them a wagon and a pair of horses. I won't attempt to describe the transfer of the boxes of books, the bedding, the bundles of provisions, while the wind blew and the rain descended. I will only say that an hour later those dripping horses looked 'real 'andsome' in the field outside my door, for the clouds had lifted, and their wet harness and steaming flanks were glistening in the sunlight.

It was quiet and calm that first evening after the rain. The lake was a kaleidoscope of changing colours from parrot-green to deepest violet. The sky was a pageant of pattern. The stems of the larch-trees beside my door shone emerald with lichen, their withered branches were flame-coloured in the evening sun. The bog was red as a robin's breast. I watched the sun drop behind lavender clouds in a saffron sky. The rushes were still; even the old dried thistle stalks did not quiver. A heron honked. A crow called 'kr-raw kr-raw,' another answered 'ke-way ke-way.'

A magpie cackled. A blackbird's last notes came down the hill. The day was done. Owls would soon be stirring. Foxes would be sniffing the scents that hang heavy in the night air.

Indoors there was only the sound of the fire. I closed my eyes and listened to its music. It seemed to me then that I had come through a curtain of rain into a land of faerie, and I was reminded how, as a child, I used to delight to go through a curtain of glass beads that hung in the corridor of my uncle's house. Beyond that curtain a door led into a scarce-used room, wherein were treasures innumerable. Fantastic shells from foreign shores. Cabinets of

*E

tropic butterflies, cases of exotic beetles, ships inside bottles. I can still hear the tinkling of the beads as I passed through the curtain. It was fairyland beyond.

That night, alone in my cottage, I feared to go to sleep lest waking I should find that it was all a dream.

My cottage is best described by the engravings, which show not only its shape but its situation. The pool itself was no more than a bog until about ninety years ago, when a Mr. Marsh built a dam across the outlet at the western end, and thereby covered some fifteen acres with water. Before the pool was formed there was deep peat in the valley. 'Oh, yes, yes; as high as your chest and higher. Well, maybe not higher than you, but higher than me.' The speaker was hardly more than five foot three to the crown of his hat. To-day the pool seems as natural as if it had been there 'for ever.'

I have made these engravings in summer for obvious reasons. At twelve hundred feet above sea-level, in winter, when the lake is silver with ice and the red bogs dusted with snow are roan as the cattle that graze there, it may be picturesque, but it is cold.

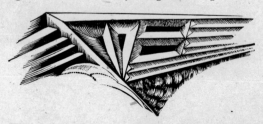

Whatever the weather there is always interest. Every day is an adventure. When there is frost the lake is covered with ice patterns that recall primitive carvings on paddle or club; rectangles, triangles, pentagons fitted together with geometric accuracy, each with a pool of clear water at its centre, a pool with bevelled sides as straight and angles as sharp as any that Euclid could have imagined. Between these scattered groups are delicate traceries that might have been drawn with a comb or surfaces that might have been scraped in soft clay by spatula or trowel, and elsewhere flocculent feathery masses like the frozen under surface of a swan's wing.

When there is snow the hills are like the flanks of some great

polar bear, and the fox and the hare leave their tracks for all to
follow; that of the fox a single, almost straight line close beside a
hedge; that of the hare across the open, a pair of long imprints
side by side, followed by two smaller pad marks one behind the
other. Like the rabbit, the hare has a kind of leap-frog action, its
hind legs coming to the ground ahead of where the forefeet have
touched. To the uninitiated it might seem that the animal was
travelling in the opposite direction.

When the day is grey and a mist shuts out everything beyond
the margin of the lake, there is silence and seclusion, and when the
south wind sighs across the
valley and purrs through the
trees, and the swish of rain on
the roof is like the rustling of
cattle among reeds, I sit by the
fire and am content to be. Rain,
sweet rain. Sweet generous
rain.

The wind is friendly up here;
the usual expressions, 'whining,'
'shrieking,' 'howling,' do not
apply. It is more like a gay
dance than a lament. However strongly it may blow across the
lake it is gay and festive, it is witty, roguish, impish, playful, but
all the time majestic, and maternal in its enfolding. Over the
water its notes are the notes of a violin, but sweeping through the
trees on the hillside it has the deep chords of a 'cello.

To-night, as I write, it is singing. It is singing the song it has
sung since the world began, it is singing the song that will ring
in these hills when the last human child is no more. Rising,
still rising, it chants and exults. All the time rising. Has the
buzzard foreknowledge? Does it sleep in the larches? Have
the mallard and widgeon found shelter? Stronger and stronger
it grows, now the fierce dance of a lover untamed. How calm
her caresses in summer. The candles are guttering. Hail crackles
on the roof and sizzles in the fire. The pine log splutters and
smoke-fringed flames wreathe upwards in star-seeking spirals to
mingle with the tresses of the wind in the dense blackness of the
night.

CHAPTER TWENTY-SIX

JACK BROWN, who brought my luggage up the hill, is brother to Bill and Maggie, who, with their mother, an old lady of ninety years, live on the other side of the mountain. They are my nearest neighbours. In the mountains of Wales the word 'neighbour' has particular significance, implying a relationship which in other parts of the world might well flatter the word 'family.' Just as in what Doughty calls 'the school and nurture of the desert' men have learnt that the first duty to a stranger is hospitality, so in the school and nurture of the mountains men have learnt that the first duty to a neighbour is helpfulness.

'Is it the loan of the horses to fetch a load of coal from the town four miles away? Is it a bit of wire for the fence? Is it a few boards to make bookshelves? Why, to be sure! Aren't we neighbours now?'

Sometimes of an evening I call for Bill and we drop down to visit James Morris at the 'Vulcan Arms' at Cwm Belan. Morris is a smith, and smiths are among the aristocracy of Wales. In medieval times they ranked with priest and bard. But Morris keeps a little 'house' beside the smithy for those who might be waiting for their horses. Sheep, lambs, tractors, and politics may be subjects of ordinary conversation there, but if you prefer it the landlord will discourse to you about astronomy or poetry or natural history, and he will bring down books from his shelves to corroborate his statements.

It was there one evening that I heard him quote from Sir James Jeans's *The Stars in their Courses*: 'The total number of stars in the universe is probably about equal to the number of drops of rain which fall on the whole of London in a day of heavy rain. . . . The average star is something like a million times as big as the earth,' and again: 'Leave only three wasps alive in the whole of Europe and the air of Europe will be more crowded with wasps than space is with stars.' Solemn thoughts with which to face the night.

Climbing the hill after closing time was not as easy as going down earlier in the evening. At about three hundred feet above the road our pace would slacken, and then Bill would become reminiscent. It was a clear moonlight night after a light fall of snow, when he told me how he had once gone shooting hares with Ted Owen. "'Twas a night like this, and about ten o'clock when Ted comes along to me. "Bill," he said, "what about a hare?"'

' "Surely," ' I said.

' "Get the gun," he said, "and come on."

'I got the gun and away we went. 'Twas a lovely night, as clear as this, only clearer. We were going up there, over that hill behind Tyn-y-fron, when what did we see but the two ears of a hare sticking up behind a gorse bush. So I up with the gun and let drive, and the hare dropped. We ran up to it and what do you think we found?'

'A rabbit,' I suggested.

'Damned if it wasn't a sheep!'

'Was she dead?'

'No, she wasn't dead, but she was badly hit about the back of the neck. "What do we do now?" says Ted.

' "Run like hell," I said. "Out of this as quick as we can." And with that we legged it hard.

'Now,' said Bill, 'I knew the farmer, so I kept out of his way, and I didn't see him for six months. I didn't see him till I walked straight into him at the fair at Llanidloes.

' "Bill," said he, "do you want to buy a sheep?"

' "No, thanks," said I. "I 'm not buying sheep."

'I didn't see him for a twelvemonth after that, and there he was with the same old ewe.

' "Bill," said he, "do you want to buy a sheep?"

' "No, thanks," said I. "I 'm not buying any sheep." Then he gave me a sharp look. "What 's the matter with that sheep?" I said. "Something wrong with her neck; a bit stiff isn't she?"

' "I 'm thinking," said he, "somebody must 'a' shot her."

' "It looks like it," I said.

' "I suppose," he said, "you have no idea who did it?"

' "I have," I said; "And I 'll tell you who did it. 'Twas I shot her," I said.

' "I knew that," he said.

' "Well, I tell thee now," I said. "I 'll buy her from thee at full market price."

'"Thee won't," he said. "I'll sell her for butcher's meat. I knew thee'd shot her. I only wanted to hear thee say thee did it."'

Another night Bill told me of a time when he and Evan Morgan were talking by the Skew Bridge over the old railway, and they saw a hare coming towards them along the track. She stopped some twenty yards short of where they were standing, and hid herself in a clump of rushes. 'Me and Evan crept up on her, and the two of us jumped on her together. Damned if she didn't skip between our legs. She didn't go far, though, before she lay down again. This time we thought to make sure of her. Damned if she didn't nip between us again. Would you believe it, a whole hour we spent trying to catch that hare? Never touched her once. Lepping about here, there, and everywhere she was, and running circles round us, and we never falling on top of anything but ourselves. "Bill," says Evan to me suddenly, "Bill," he says, "this is no hare." "By damn, I think you're right," I said. "Come on," I said. "I'm for home." And we left her there. If Evan had 'a' kept his mouth shut we'd 'a' been there still. And we wouldn't 'a' caught her neither.'

It is not only in Wales but in many other parts of the British Isles that witches are thought capable of taking the form of a hare.

Bill lives at Bwlchhafodygog, which means: 'The Pass Beside the Summer Home of the Cuckoo.' That is half a mile to the east of my cottage, Glanrhyd, which means: 'The Shore by the Ford.' I have another neighbour, by name Clifford Holmes, who lives at Rhydyronen, meaning 'The Ford by the Ash,' about a mile to the west. To get to his place you have to cross a few acres of bog, follow a sheep track along the edge of a mountain, clamber down a precipice, and wade a river. Then you are nearly there.

'Make the place your own,' said Holmes. 'Any day you like, any meal you like. No,' he added, 'don't come for a meal, come for the day; come after breakfast and we'll see you home before midnight.' A dog, or a gun, or a pony, anything I wanted I could have for the asking.

It was after a midday meal one Sunday that he asked if I'd like to go for a walk on the mountain behind his house.

'I would,' I said, 'but I'd rather do it another day, for I'm crippled with lumbago. I think it must be all the hill climbing that has brought it on,' I said, 'though indeed I've been troubled

with it for a year or more. I think that precipice to-day has
touched it up a bit more than usual.'

'You should see George,' he said.

'Who 's George?' I asked.

'George Lloyd. He 's a farmer near here.'

'He 'd cure you,' said Mrs. Holmes.

'Where will I see him?' I asked.

'Go up and tell George I want him,' said Holmes to his son.

'He 'll cure you surely,' said Mrs. Holmes.

Ten minutes later Lloyd appeared, a middle-aged man with quiet
grey eyes. He sat down by the open hearth and for half an hour
we talked of everything except my complaint.

'This man has lumbago,' said Holmes at last.

'Has he?' said George.

'I 've had it a year or more,' I said, 'and it 's painful.'

'What brought it on, d' you think?' he asked.

'A relation of mine,' I said; 'a strong-minded female, who put
me to cut down the biggest tree in her garden with the smallest
axe in the country.'

'Did you fell it?' asked Mrs. Holmes.

'I did,' I said.

'Well, now!' she said sympathetically.

'Could you cure him, George?' asked Holmes.

'I could,' said George.

'Will you cure him?' asked Holmes.

'I will,' said George.

'Where will you do it?' asked Mrs. Holmes.

'In the back kitchen,' said George.

We went into the back kitchen, hung with saddles and spurs and
sheep shears. George took off his coat and rolled up his sleeves.

'What is your name?' he asked me; 'your full name?'

I told him.

Meanwhile Mrs. Holmes had produced a ball of darning wool.
George took hold of the extreme end of the yarn, and tied a knot
on it. Mrs. Holmes stood about three yards away from him, and
the wool was stretched taut between them. George repeated my
name in full. Then he ran his finger and thumb along the first
eighteen inches of the yarn, and in almost the same movement
fitted the knot against the point of his bare elbow. From there

to the point of his second finger he measured out a length of the wool and, from the point reached, a second and a third length in the same way. Mrs. Holmes marked the spot indicated by the third measurement. Then, beginning again, the whole operation was repeated. By this time the measure proved to be an inch and a half longer than at first.

'You've got it,' said George to me.

'If you hadn't the pains, his finger would have fallen short the second time,' said Mrs. Holmes.

'I could nearly tell by the feel of the yarn in my fingers,' said George.

The operation was then performed a third time, with a result similar to the second.

George then snapped off the wool at the point where Mrs. Holmes was holding it. He folded it in two, and then again and again, finally wrapping it in a piece of brown paper.

'Take this with you,' he said, 'and tie it around your left leg next to the skin. Don't let it drop. Handle it carefully. Let it stay till it comes off by itself. Burn it when it comes off. How long are you staying?' he added.

'Another week,' I told him.

'You 'll be better before you go,' he said.

I went back to my cottage and did as I had been told. Those of you who buy coloured water from chemists, and those of you who feel the better for merely pressing a bell in Harley Street, may smile when I tell you that the pain was much better next morning, that within a week it had disappeared, and that it hasn't come back since.

But I 'm not cutting down any more trees with blunt axes for a while.

CHAPTER TWENTY-SEVEN

I HAVE GREAT TROUBLE with my housework owing to the interruptions. It isn't that many people come to see me, but that whenever I begin to do a job inside the house there is always something sure to happen outside that catches the tail of my eye. It often takes me two hours to make my bed. For instance, one morning, as I was turning the mattress, I noticed a heron on the ice. It was within fifty yards of my window, so when I took up my glasses I could see every feather on it. It was walking circumspectly, like the proverbial cat on the wall, and I watched to see what would happen if its weight proved too much for the ice. Its movements were the epitome of stalking. As each foot came down it was, at the last moment, slid forward just an inch further than one had expected before it touched the ice. The precise movements of its toes were like a slow-motion picture, as with each step they hung together when lifted and spread out again when they were about to touch the surface. While I watched the heron saw a fish. The long legs came together. The bird leaned forward. Its head stuck out and further out. Still further the beak protruded until, just as the bird was about to strike, its legs slid backwards from under it, and it fell on its chest with a flop on the ice. It got up, somewhat ruffled in its dignity, but in no way frightened. Then it walked sedately to the bank. I went back to my bedmaking. But as I was shaking the pillows I saw a kestrel pass the window and perch in a larch-tree close by. First on the extreme tip of the tree it sat, and afterwards on a twig of one of the branches. It sat there, fluffed up, looking as innocent as a thrush. Yet all the time its eyes were searching the ground. Twice within a few minutes it swooped into the gorse at the foot of the trees, but each time it missed its quarry. After the second failure it went away.

I got busy with my blankets. But the heron was back again on the ice. At first it took more care than before, but the sight of a big fish was too much for it. It struck hard. Instead of piercing the fish its beak skidded sideways on the ice, and the bird landed heavily on its head. This time it was thoroughly shaken. It lay there dishevelled. Then with difficulty it rose to its feet, and after resting for a while, as if stunned, it walked slowly to the shelter of a sallow-tree, where it remained for an hour or more, hunched up with its head between its shoulders. It did no more fishing that day.

The force with which herons strike at a big fish must be considerable. They seem to put the whole weight of their body behind it. For a smaller one they make a more dainty jab. The big ones they take ashore for a formal meal, the smaller ones are just rolled over a few times in the bill, and then flicked down the throat. A shake of the head helps the victims in the right direction.

On that same day there were goldfinches feeding on the sunny slope above the lake, and fieldfares chittering in the storm-swept alders. Next morning a light fall of snow rested on the frozen surface of the lake. No whiter cloth was ever laid. Throughout the day it shone immaculate. But towards evening the wind veered to the south. Then came the rain, and soon the glory of the whiteness was lost.

At dawn next day the hills and the sky were all one leaden grey. The lake had thawed, and the goosanders were back on the water. Of all our ducks these must be amongst the handsomest, the drake with his dark green head, black back, and ivory breast and sides suffused with tints of salmon, the ducks with chestnut heads, grey backs, and the same flushed breast; both of them with crimson bill. It is a wonderful sight to see a dozen of them, in a great phalanx, swimming at full speed down the lake, throwing out long silver ripples to some thirty yards behind them. Their speed and the ease with which they dive recall the activities of dolphins, and there is the same joyous expression in their faces. It seems that for the most part they swallow the smaller of their prey as they catch them under the water, but often they bring a larger one to the surface before disposing of it. Then with it well down in the gullet the bird rises on its tail in the water, and flaps its wings violently as if to shake it further down. Next moment it has dived again.

They are incessantly diving. In shallow water they appear again almost immediately, though always a little ahead of where

one had expected them, but in deep water they may stay below the surface for as long as a minute or more. The late Dr. J. M. Dewar calculated that there is not only a constant ratio between their time under water and the depth of the water in which they are diving, but also between the time under water and the time on the surface between dives.

Their power of instantaneous and, when in groups, simultaneous diving is astonishing, showing a capacity for quick decisions far beyond anything of the kind that we possess, and beside which trained athletes leaping to the pistol shot would seem awkward and lumbering.

The heron finds the activities of the goosanders helpful to its own fishing. When the bottom has been disturbed small fish are more likely to be in evidence, as they dart from stone to stone in search of new shelter. With its long slow strides the heron is, of course, quite unable to keep up with the rapid swimming of the ducks, even though at times it breaks into an ungainly run. It is, therefore, compelled to fly here and there across the pool, endeavouring always, and as often as not unsuccessfully, to anticipate their next sphere of activity. When the ducks are present in numbers they pay little attention to their neighbour, but when one of them is there alone it seems glad of companionship. The duck will then fish close in to where the heron is standing, while the tall bird stands motionless, with neck outstretched, on the alert for anything that may be disturbed. I have seen this go on for nearly an hour, the duck sometimes sitting close up to the heron, almost touching it, as though the two were happy to be in each other's company.

When the pochard and tufted duck come in it is a sign of storm. One day fourteen of the latter swept down to the pool. Through

a wide crescent curve they flew over the edge of the lake, then down they came, down, down, till thrusting their heads upwards and throwing out their feet they ploughed deep silver furrows in the water. There is wonderful precision in the way a tufted duck alights on the water. While they circle in the air their feet are straight behind them, close to their body, but as they near the surface the feet drop slightly. Then in a series of quick movements the toes open, the feet swing forward sharply, up tilt the toes, and the flat soles of the feet, sinking into the water, almost at right angles, brake the flight of the bird.

The day that those duck came in there were cross-currents of wind from the south and the south-west, so that the surface of the lake was blown into interlacing wavelets resembling the scale formation on a fish. Hills were grey as the sky. They became indistinguishable from the sky, but for the dark lines of the hedges. Towards evening fitful gleams of light brought the mountains nearer at one moment and drove them further away at the next. The world seemed coloured like an old tin can, a tin that gleams in the sun, but has rusty edges, rust the colour of the bogs that edged the lake.

In the evening the rain came. Water spluttered under my door

and splashed through the leads of my window. But there was
fire in the hearth, bright blazing fire. I took down Burns's *Poems*.

'When Januar' wind was blawin' cauld,
    As to the north I took my way,
The mirksome night did me enfauld,
    I knew na whare to lodge till day.

By my good luck a maid I met,
    Just in the middle o' my care;
And kindly she did me invite
    To walk into a chamber fair. . . .

She made the bed baith large and wide,
    Wi' twa white hands she spread it down;
She put the cup to her rosy lips,
    And drank: "Young man, now sleep ye soun'."

She snatch'd the candle in her hand,
    And frae my chamber went wi' speed;
But I call'd her quickly back again
    To lay some mair below my head. . . .

Her hair was like the links o' gowd,
    Her teeth were like the ivorie;
Her cheeks like lilies dipt in wine,
    The lass that made the bed to me.

Her bosom was the driven snaw,
    Twa drifted heaps sae fair to see;
Her limbs the polish'd marble stane,
    The lass that made the bed to me.'

And I to be living alone,

CHAPTER TWENTY-EIGHT

ONE OF THE DISADVANTAGES of living alone is that it leads to a neglect of meals. It is dull work cooking for oneself, as dull as drinking good wine alone. We are apt to make do with a few scraps or even to go without. I remember a time, some years ago, when I was 'doing for' myself. Something seemed to have gone wrong in my inside. There was that sinking feeling in the pit of the stomach, a coldness about the ribs, a general weariness, a distaste for food. Must have eaten something that disagreed, I thought. Better lay off food for a day or two. But I was no better next day, and the following day I was worse still. You 've caught a chill, I said to myself. Then I began to consider what was the best treatment for a chill. A hot drink, of course, but there was only water in the house. I decided that I must risk a visit to the 'Star.' So I put on an overcoat and a muffler and away I went, thinking to have a drop or two of whisky. But when I got inside the bar the first thing I saw on the shelf was a bottle of rum, Lemon Hart rum at that. Just as a dog knows when to eat grass I knew that that was the stuff for me at that particular moment, so I bought the bottle and went home. Then I boiled up the kettle and I mixed myself a good stiff drink. When I had drunk it I felt better. I repeated the treatment, and I felt better still. Then I mixed myself a third. When I was half-way through this I suddenly said to myself, I 'm hungry. Damn it, I said, I 'm mad hungry. So I looked about the place to see what I had in the way of food, and I found eight eggs. I dropped the lot into the kettle that was still on the hob, and when they were boiled I ate them. I was instantly cured. Never felt better in my life. All I had wanted was food. I went to bed and slept well, and woke in the morning as fresh as a skylark in May.

I was reminded of all this one morning at my lake when I felt a touch of emptiness about the ribs. Better take no risks, I said. I wanted coal anyway. So off I went to the town of Llanidloes. Two miles out I overtook Jim Williams, who was driving a cow to the market. He was singing when I caught up on him.

'My hands work hard for others, but my lips are kept for thee,
And that 's what Maggie whispers when she comes to visit me.'

136

Jim is a gay enough lad, and knows the full use of his dark eye-lashes when there 's a girl about.

'Haven't you got a woman up there yet?' he asked.

'I have not,' I said.

'Maybe you 're going to meet one now at the station?'

'I 'm going in to order a bit of coal to keep me warm,' I told him.

'That 's cheaper in the long run,' he said.

'Go on with your singing,' I said.   Then he broke into song again:

'The sun is always shining, now Maggie stays with me.
We 've been to church and paid the clerk his 'gitimizing fee,
And the wild duck swims across the lake with ducklings three
        times three.
It 's ambitious, but we 'll try it, is what Maggie says to me.'

'I had a dog once that could sing as well as a Christian,' said Jim.   'A spaniel, black and white.   His name was Sam.   He 'd sit up on the table in the kitchen and I 'd pitch him the note, and he 'd howl right on it.   He 'd follow me up and down the scale, howling all the time.   Nearly drove me mother mad, thinking 'twould bring death on the place.   And I tell you too, that dog could drive the pony.   Well, if he couldn't he could hold it. He 'd sit up on the driver's seat and I 'd put the reins in his mouth. If that pony started to move Sam would pull him in tight.   Didn't matter if it was the station or anywhere else, Sam would hold him. Only one place he wouldn't take the reins, outside the "Stag."'

'You stayed in there too long,' I suggested.

'No,' he said, 'the dog liked his beer; the boss would always give him a drop.   I tell you another thing too,' he added; 'if I was out with the gun and the farmer came out after the shot, and I had to run for it before I 'd picked up the bird, that dog would mark the bird and go out by himself after dark and fetch it in.'

'Did you know that sheep-dog belonged to my uncle?' asked Jack Griffiths, who had joined us.

'The big old one that was crippled with rheumatism?' said Jim.

'That 's him.   He 's dead now.'

'Old age, I suppose?'

'No.   He was a killer.'

'A killer!'

'At it for weeks. Killed twenty sheep in one night just for sport. Nipped 'em in the gullet.'

'But he couldn't hardly walk across the yard.'

'That 's what we thought, till a week come Friday. Me and Tom Lewis was up that mornin'. We 'd been up several mornin's. He 'd lost a dozen. We 'd lost twice that, countin' lambs. We was up t' see if we could catch who 'd been at it. Would you believe it? There was that stiff old dog—well, we thought he was a stiff old dog—running as free as a fox, roundin' 'em up into a corner, he was, and springin' at 'em ag'in the fence. Tom showed hisself at the bottom of the field, and the dog jumped into the lane at the top. He didn't see me till he saw the gun, and after that he didn't see nothing any more. Would you believe it? Laying in the house all day pretendin'; killin' sheep all night. Once they start nothin' will stop 'em.'

'I reckon one taste of blood and they 're finished,' said Jim.

As we went along we were met by others who appeared from side roads, and from farms adjoining the main roads, all going in the same direction. One man had a couple of yearling bullocks, another had a two-year-old heifer, a third had a cow and a calf. We overtook a calf that refused to walk. It eventually drove to the market in style, in the back seat of an Austin Twelve. I was introduced to two brothers, both of them little men. 'He 's had better grazing nor we,' said the elder, looking me up and down. I was reminded of my old tailor in Cork who, after an interval of several years, was measuring me for a suit of clothes. 'Begod you 've put a hape of mate on you,' he said.

On reaching the fair ground the cattle were sorted into pens, and a man went round among them daubing their hind quarters with paste, to which the owners attached numbered tickets supplied by the auctioneer. Everywhere there were farmers appraising and dispraising the beasts. Among the cows possible purchasers were testing the udders and running their hands over the animals' bellies to see if the veins were taut. A full udder and slack veins signified little, the cow might not have been milked for some time; but a full udder and full veins meant that she was a good milker. There were pens of sheep too—a line of sheep-dogs were tied to the railing on the edge of the fair ground—and a solitary bull, a huge smooth-skinned animal held not only by a pole to the nose, but by a rope from the fore fetlock that passed through a girth behind the shoulders, and then between the creature's hind legs, so that at any moment it could be tripped.

'Quiet as a chicken,' I was told. 'The law compels all that harness when the beasts are being driven through the streets.'

After the sale I found myself talking to 'Old Dan,' a drover. 'I 'm like the cuckoo,' he said, 'here to-day and gone to-morrow.' He had known Jim's father in the army. 'Bin old sweats together.' That was in the South African War. 'Slope hipe! Order hipe! Present hipe!' He could do them all. ''Ad the 'andcuffs on too; 'ands be'ind the back. Phew! Glad to 'ave someone wipe the so-and-so flies off yer so-and-so face. Twenty-one years in the army.'

He was tall and lean. His eyes were watery, his face was red, and the corners of his mouth turned down. His cap hung over one side of his head, as if balanced on one ear. He was the sort that would always be 'moved on.' Yet, to his pals, 'Old Dan is all right. Never do you down. Give you his last farthing.' His appearance reminded me of a man I knew in the army whose crime-sheet was so black that the colonel decided that there were only two courses open. One was to discharge him with ignominy from the service, the other was to promote him to sergeant and put him in charge of the defaulters. He decided on the latter course, and from that day the man was a shining light in the battalion.

Dan is a good drover, looks after his beasts. 'When he 's on the job he 's on the job. A sight better principled nor many as passes him on the road.'

At the sales he seems to know before the auctioneer when the bidding is over. 'Open out, gentlemen! Open out!' is his call. Then, as the hammer falls, and the beast, prodded on either side by sticks, lurches through the crowd, Dan ushers in the next lot through a gap on the other side of the pen.

CHAPTER TWENTY-NINE

THE CLOSER I AM to nature the happier I am. I love to be alone with the winds that come up from the other side of the world, to be alone with these hills, some of the oldest on our planet. I like to feel the seasonal rhythm, to be conscious of the rising sap in spring, the maturing of the growth in summer, the tonic of the autumn, the sleep of winter.

I thought when I came to my cottage by the lake that I was coming to find peace in solitude. I thought to hear no sound but the cry of the birds, the trickle of the stream through the bog, the breathing of the wind, the crackle of the fire. And so I lived for a time, grudging each moment when a fellow human drew near, counting only those moments happy when I was alone, until the last day of the year. That night there came visitors, farmers and shepherds, with their wives and their daughters. They sat with me around my fire, and as naturally as the logs took light so their voices took fire, and they sang song after song in their native tongue. The eyes of the old men were closed while their hands beat time to the music. The eyes of the young girls were open but their thoughts were far away. Then I realized that they were born of the same soil as the reeds and the rushes, and that their voices were the spirits of the wind and the rain and the sun that shines golden on the snow. Then I realized too that I need no longer be alone or lonely, for here were men and women who loved the things that I loved, men whose roots were as deep in the soil as those of the gnarled alder-trees on the hillside, women whose hearts were fresh as the starwort in the well. Dai was among the party, and before they left they sang a song which seemed to tear deep into the vitals of one's emotions. I said to Dai: 'It has the notes of a harp.' He said to me: 'It *is* The Golden Harp.' Then they went out into the crisp night air and I was glad that it was dark, for there were tears in my eyes. I found it difficult to speak. At last, in an effort to break the tension, I said to Dai: 'That's the hell of a bright star over the hill, have you any idea what its name is?' 'I dunno,' he said, 'it's been there for years.'

And so with the fun that was in their hearts they disappeared into the black belt of fir-trees that straddles the hill.

Hundreds of millions of years ago the sea deposited layer after layer of silt which in the course of ages became hardened into rock, and in the course of still further ages was once again dis-integrated, this time into pebbles. Millions of years after this a

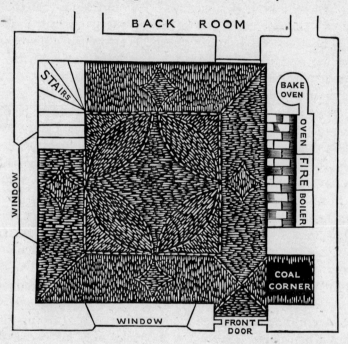

biped mammal, naked save for the wool of other animals, saw these stones and took pleasure in them. With that liking for formal pattern which distinguishes him from other creatures, he set himself to adorn the floor of his shelter with these stones. With all-unconscious art he created order out of chaos, and many generations looking upon it since then have seen that it is good.

I have already mentioned 'pitched' floors, once a regular feature of Welsh houses, but now frowned upon by sanitary inspectors. As if carpets were sanitary! The pattern of my floor is shown in the engraving. You who live insulated from the earth by carpets over under-felts over boards on joists laid on concrete may smile at me whose bare feet touch with joy these age-old stones, but I have a joy in my heart that sings the song that the south wind sings among the grasses of the hills, the song that the west wind whispers to the answering ripples of the lake.

It is a pity that the Christian religion reserves its precept 'earth to earth' for the dead.   Far better if they preached it to the living.

It has been said that: 'The longing to be primitive is a disease of culture; it is archaism in morals.   To be so preoccupied with vitality is a symptom of anaemia.'   I would reply that the man, to-day, who is not conscious of his physical imperfections must not only be diseased but in many respects atrophied.   Thoreau was right when he said: 'If a man does not keep step with his companions it may be because he hears a different drummer.'   Some people would have us all march to the same tune.   It is as if they insisted that the waltz, the tango, and the hula should all be danced to the same music.   Second thoughts, they'd probably stop the hula, and the tango too.   It isn't very long since some people tried to stop the waltz.   'Ask the father before the movings of ambition have calcined his heart . . . if he would commit the innocence of his child to the pollution of the waltz?   Ask the mother, before the demon of fashion has taken possession of her feelings, and shut her eyes to the unhallowed nature of many of the rites— ask her, can she consent to commit her daughter promiscuously to the arms of each waltzer? . . . Ask the lover . . . could he endure the sight of the adopted of his heart half-embraced and all but reclining in the arms of another?   Could he endure to see, which is often seen, the impassioned glance of a stranger turn upon those beauties which were believed to be exclusively his own?—could he bear to witness her lips (which, if he has approached at all, it has been almost with a sentiment of adoration) approach near enough to those of each man who may be a waltzer,

If not to touch, to taint?'

That is from a *Ladies' Pocket Book of Etiquette*, dated 1838.

CHAPTER THIRTY

FOR TEN WEEKS I was away from the Wye. I walked the cloisters, and wore a gown at dinner. Then, at last, towards the end of March, I got my collar off in the hills. The sallows were silvering, the birches were purpling, the blackthorns were whitening, the small hard buds on the broom were softening to a brighter green. 'Broom is good for the kidneys,' I was told. 'If you 're having trouble with them boil up a few sprigs in water and drink a wineglassful of the liquid in the morning. It acts on the kidneys like an onion to the eyes. It 's good for the dropsy of the legs too. Soak your feet in a bath of the hot liquid. It works wonders.'

The larches were speckled with crimson, the tips of the gorse shone gold. Soft green rosettes of the foxgloves were starring the hillside. Small birds were establishing the boundaries of their nesting territory, yellow-hammers and linnets in the gorse to the east, hedge sparrows in the gorse to the west, chaffinches in the hedge beside the house. Wheatears were frisking on the clods of fresh-ploughed soil.

The heron had disappeared. No doubt she was down among the tree tops in the valley. She would have gone there in answer to her mate who might have been calling for days. Then there would have been caressing of each other's plumage with their long bills, and he would have brought her sticks and grown excited while she put them in place, either on top of last year's nest or to make a new one. By the end of March they would have been taking turns at sitting on their four or five greeny-blue eggs, or indeed they might already have been rifling the streams and ponds to feed their squawking youngsters.

The ducks had gone too, though a cormorant put in an occasional appearance. I can only suppose that the goosanders were away on some Highland loch, thinking of possible nesting sites in hollow trees or sheltered nooks among boulders or maybe mere holes in the ground. The drakes would be displaying themselves to the ducks, rising in the water and pointing downwards with their crimson bills to their salmon-tinted breasts. They would be splashing up water with their feet, they would be swimming round and round the ducks, bowing to them and spasmodically chasing them, until sinking low with neck outstretched along the water each female would invite her chosen to the marriage ceremony.

Their place on my lake was taken by black-headed gulls, who were busy with their courting. Along the edge of the water they spent their days, in pairs, sidling up to each other with wings slightly opened, posturing with head thrown low and beak turned upwards, pecking at each other's feathers, dipping their beaks in the water as if to drink. Sometimes the male would find a worm or other morsel, and offer it to the female who, accepting it, would later give him his reward.

Curlews have come in from the coast, and now, day and night,  the hills resound with their cries. The red-shank has been called the Warden of the Marshes, and for the same reason the curlew might well be called the Warden of the Hills. Through my telescope I watched one across the lake. Though seemingly resting, with its head over its shoulder, and its long curved beak tucked in among the feathers on its back, its eyes were open, and all the time its body rotated from side to side, slowly and regularly like the wheel pendulum of a clock, so that on either side an eye covered all possible sources of danger.

And if curlews were there in numbers so also were lambs. Whereas the spring of 1941 had been one of the worst within living memory, that of 1942 was one of the best. In 1941 the spring had seemed non-existent. There was snow on the mountains late into April. The wind blew from the east continuously. Whether the sky was clear or hazy there was that same knife that cut into your bones. There were times when it didn't even drop in the evening. On and on it went for days and weeks, and it seemed for months. There was scarcely a leaf on the trees when April faded into May. There was still no grass for the ewes. The hills were yellow with drought, the lambs were pinched and dying. But in 1942 there had been little snow and the ewes were in good condition. Even if there had been gales during the lambing season they were soft winds from the south that brought the new grass. Lambs were everywhere, leaping, capering, bounding, instinctively practising all those movements which in a wild state would have been an everyday necessity of maturity.

In his *Childhood of Animals* Chalmers Mitchell, describing how the games of young animals bear a definite relation to their later life, writes:

'Animals that have to escape or catch their prey by swiftness and dexterity rush madly in circles, or race each other until they have to lie down from exhaustion. Goat, sheep, and chamois are mountainous, rock-loving animals, accustomed to make high vertical jumps from one ledge to another. Their kids and lambs practise high jumps with an effect that is ludicrous when we see them on flat ground suddenly springing into the air. Rocky-mountain goats are said to be the most sure-footed of all animals; they are slow and deliberate in their movements, creeping along almost invisible ledges on the face of precipitous cliffs. Their kids show the same stealthy and careful movement, climbing to the roof of their shelter, not by sudden jumps, but almost inch by inch. Gazelles and antelopes which inhabit open plains practise long jumps when they are young. Young dogs and wolves run round and round in circles trying to head each other off. Most of the smaller cats are accustomed to take almost vertical high jumps; domestic kittens can be seen to make sudden leaps in the air almost like young goats.'

So with ourselves, the boy is father to the man, and, in spite of some recent efforts to the contrary, the girl remains the mother to the woman. Some years ago I knew a mother who had the idea that the difference of interests shown by boys and girls was due entirely to outside suggestion. She wanted her daughter to be on equal terms with the child's brothers, and rightly so, but, unfortunately, she mistook the meaning of the word 'equal' for that of the word 'identical.' For that reason the child was not allowed to see a doll. The boys didn't have them, why should the girl? It was only putting her on the straight road to subjection. And thus the child was brought up until, in the fourth or fifth year of her age, a visitor arrived at the house in the absence of the mother. Being entirely ignorant of her crime she presented the child with a doll. Then, indeed, there was commotion. The child was entranced. Never had she seen anything so wonderful in her life. Her instant delight and the hours of loving care after-wards lavished on that doll were a final answer to all the theories on the subject. The mother admitted herself beaten, and I'm not sure that in her heart she wasn't glad of it.

One morning some ewes were lying on the grass under my window. One of them seemed a bit restless. Every now and then she would get up and lie down again. She would stretch her head out along the ground, rubbing her neck on the grass, then she would continue her cud-chewing. I looked up from my engraving, after a short interval, to see a new-born lamb tottering to its feet.

'It seems very easy,' I said to a farmer.

'That's nothing,' he said. 'My brother went down the other night to give the mare a bit of hay. When he got to the stable she was feeding happy enough. When he came down from the loft with an armful of hay, not five minutes later, she had a foal standing beside her.'

On rough days a shepherd boy might bring a lamb into my cottage to warm it by the fire. 'She brought twins, and this one is a bit weak,' he would tell me. Then we would give it a drop of milk from a bottle, through a quill in the cork, and afterwards he would tuck it inside his coat and take it back to its mother.

But when the sun shone and the earth began to dry I would wander over the sheep-terraced hills, and watch the men of the soil mastering the soil. On these uneven slopes they sow by hand. One handful of corn to each step the sower casts from the hopper on his arm as he walks to and fro across the field, guided by the sticks he has stuck in the ground to form lines eight paces apart. And, as he covers each strip with seed, the harrow follows, burying the grain under the soil. In a week's time a light roller will make it all compact.

As I wander by the hedgerows I surprise the yellow-hammers. the tits, the warblers who have come back to nest in the high lands. Or it may be a linnet, who is carrying a mouthful of dry grass to its nest. Seeing me it turns aside and perches on a twig, eyeing me carefully for a while. I try to appear uninterested, but it sees through my pretence. It flits to the top of a gorse bush, watches again for a while, then opening its beak it lets the fragments of grass blow away in the wind as if to say: 'You didn't *really* think I was building, did you?' Then it flies up the hillside.

It may be a hare that I surprise. She sits up and looks at me for a moment, then away she lollops, climbing the hillside with long galloping strides. Her ears are erect until she reaches the crest of the slope, then down they go and her body too, belly to the ground, for the few moments that she shows against the sky-line.

Wrens and robins are in the hedgerows, the wren who, for some sin of long ago, must ever fly through a hedge and never over it, and the robin who, for a like offence, must never go through, but always over. I like Joseph Blagrave's remarks when, writing in 1675, he says: 'Concerning the Jenny-Wren, I hold the little creature to be à curious fine Song-Bird. He is of a fine chearful Nature, and singeth sweetly and delightsomely, none exceeding him for the nature of the song he sings. This bird builds twice a year, first about the latter end of April, and makes her Nest with dry Moss and Leaves . . . leaving but one little hole to go in and out at; she lays abundance of Eggs, I have had eighteen out of one Nest, which would seem very strange, if it were not a thing so generally common. It's to admiration how so small a little-bodied Bird can cover so great a company of Eggs; I am persuaded the Cock and Hen sit both together; but when they have hatched, to feed so great a company and not to miss one bird, and in the dark also, 'tis a very curious thing to consider.'

Blagrave was depending more on romantic imagination than on direct observation when he pictured the cock and hen sitting side by side on their profusion of eggs. Recent evidence seems to show that incubation is by the hen alone; indeed, there seems little evidence that the cock even helps in feeding the youngsters until after they have left the nest. Of this stump-tailed little bird, dear to every one's heart, I cannot refrain from quoting the late T. A. Coward, whose *Birds of the British Isles* must have seen the lining of many a tweed jacket: 'It is so small and mouse-like, so easily lost sight of when it is hunting for food, that many count it rare. It is everywhere, from the tops of the highest moors to the sea-coast. Its movements as it creeps or climbs are incessant rather than rapid; its short flights swift but not sustained; its tiny round wings whirr with misty vibration as they carry it from bush to bush. It is a bird of the breezy uplands, even in winter; it will

F

slip amongst the wiry stems of the heather when snow lies thick above, vanishing into gloomy caves, a troglodyte indeed. It frequents the gardens, hopping about the flower-beds, or disappearing suddenly behind the ivy on the walls; in the farm and stack-yard it examines every nook and cranny for hidden insects; but it is quite as abundant in the thick woods, alike amongst the tree roots and tangled undergrowth. The rushes round the meres harbour a few in winter; these marshy spots provide food when other places fail.'

Like the birds returning, one day a reed bunting, the next a sandpiper, the next a flycatcher, so each day a new flower appears in the bogs or in the lanes. The needle whin, modest cousin of the gorse, sparkling amid the close-cropped heather; the cotton grass, known up here as 'silk of the moors,' the greater celandine beside the cottages, marigolds beside the streams, vetches, orchids, yellow rattle, and the little blue milkwort, whose presence in a pasture was once thought to increase the milk yield of the cattle grazing there.

On the hillside the hard fern and the male fern unroll beside the crosiers of the bracken. As I pass among the gorse bushes a linnet slips quietly from her nest, through the thorny scrub, only emerging from cover some thirty yards away; a yellow-hammer, less prudent, flushes at my approach, leaving her purple-scribbled eggs in their hair-lined nest. Within a dozen days those fragile shells will have given place to yellow-edged gaping mouths responsive to every tremor of the branches. Within a dozen weeks the same naked helpless young will be fledged and fending for themselves. Within as many months they will be among the brightest jewels of the hedgerows.

And how spotless those nests are. Many people do not realize the unremitting care on the part of most parent birds to keep their nests clean. It was probably Gilbert White who first drew attention to the subject in this country. Writing of the house martin he said: 'At first when the young are hatched, and are in a naked and helpless condition, the parent birds with tender assiduity, carry out what comes from their young. Was it not for this affectionate cleanliness the nestlings would soon be burnt up, and destroyed in so deep and hollow a nest, by their own caustic excrement.' Speaking generally, in the first few days after hatching, when there is little more than a secretion from the young birds, whatever passes is swallowed by the parents, but after that, when normal digestion has begun, the faeces are carried away by the parent birds and dropped at some distance from the nest. As if designed to help the parents the excrement at this stage is enclosed in a gelatinous capsule 'and therefore is the easier conveyed off without soiling or daubing.'

Recently I watched a pair of starlings carrying food to their young in a hole in a tree. Every time that either of them came out of the nest it carried a white pellet in its beak. Many people are surprised at how soon human babies can learn cleanly habits. What would they think if they could see young birds, of four and five days old, co-operating with their parents in a similar purpose? One observer has told how he saw a blue tit, in a crowded nest, raise its posterior in such a way that it was standing on its beak and feet like a three-legged stool. The parent bird then took the capsule direct from its cloaca. Similar behaviour has been recorded of young whitethroats. The majority of young birds excrete the pellet on to the rim of the nest, where it can be the more easily seen by the parent, and some even have definite areas on the rim to which they resort with regularity.

As an instance of the care with which parent birds dispose of such excreta, the dipper has been seen not only to put the droppings of its young into the stream, but to take them out again if caught in an eddy and drop them in again where the current was flowing more directly.

There are, of course, exceptions to this general rule of nest cleanliness. Many of the waders and ducks who leave the nest soon after hatching take no trouble at all. Any one who has lingered under a heron's or a sparrow-hawk's nest may have realized that the nestlings of these birds have their own private methods of shooting their excrement from the nest.

Now, when in one field the corn is showing green, and in another the 'taters' have been ploughed in, a third is being got ready for the turnips, and a fourth for a bit of rape for the sheep. Then the horses will be turned out to grass until the hay harvest.

'Did you see that horse old Williams tried to sell me?' asked Bill. 'Pull? That horse couldn't pull the skin off a rice pudding.'

And while the horses are enjoying their rest, men are busy with the sheep. The lambs must be ear-marked, and then the sheep washed before they are shorn during the last week of June. Just as there is a heraldry of raddle by which every farm has its blazoning of red, blue, or black on shoulders, back, or rump of the sheep, so each owner has a distinctive mark punched in the ear of his lambs. It may be in the right ear, it may be in the left, it may be in both. It may be in the tip of the ear, it may be in the side. It may be a single notch, it may be two notches, or it may be a small hole punched right through. One register that I saw showed over a thousand variations from a few simple brands. When we consider that it is possible with only two different marks to get fifteen different badges of ownership we see what an infinity there can be when the motifs are more varied.

CHAPTER THIRTY-ONE

'This BUSINESS OF BOOK READING is very interesting,' said Ted Owen, in the 'Vulcan' one night.

'I never read anything that I can avoid,' I said.

'But I thought you wus a professor?'

'A lecturer,' I corrected.

'Doesn't you have to read?'

'My grannie is for ever reading love stories,' said the youngest member of the party.

'I reckon reading books is letting someone else do the thinking for you,' said an old man in the corner.

'Some books help you to think,' I said. 'They are the ones to read.'

'He's right,' said Ted.

'By God he is,' said the landlord.

'I came across a book th' other day,' said Ted, 'tells how they hung a bull on the gallows for murdering a man.'

'On a gallows?' asked Jack Evans, who'd just been fined for poaching.

'On a gallows, yes, same as you or me. Well, same as you, not me. There was a sow, too, another time. In France it was. They tried her before the judge after she'd gored a child. Dressed her up in a man's clothes, and hanged her in the public square. Yes, and the hangman got a new pair o' gloves same as if she'd been a Christian.'

'Daft,' said Jack.

'Well, of course it's daft, but it's true.'

'Nonsense!'

'It's not nonsense,' said the landlord. '' Tisn't so long since they took a bull up on the hill behind here and cut him to pieces 'cause he'd gored a man. Wouldn't sell him for butcher's meat; said he was tainted.'

'And there was rats,' continued Ted, 'had been eatin' the barley. They put a lawyer on to them.'

'A hell of a lot of good he'd do.'

'He prosecuted them.'

'Did he bring 'em into court?'

'Well, how could he? But they gave 'em a lawyer to defend theyselves.'

'Poor man's counsel they call that,' suggested Jack.

'Lies,' said the old man in the corner.

''Tisn't lies. It 's in the book,' said Ted.

'The book is a liar.'

'Well, I 'm only tellin' you. It 's in the book. The judge said if you 's going to put 'em in the dock you must 'a' someone to defend 'em. It 's only fair, he says. So they fixed up with a barrister to act for 'em. What 's more, he got 'em off.'

'Got 'em off?'

'Yes, got 'em off. Said his clients couldn't obey the writ without danger to their lives, too many cats and dogs about the place, said no defendant bound to appear in court at peril of his life.'

'I s'pose they 'd 'a' called the priest in to give 'em the oath.'

'They called the priest in to put a curse on some slugs was eating their gardens.'

'Well, doesn't they call in the clergy to lay spirits?'

'This was the bishop, an' he excommunicated them.'

'Well, I 'll be damned.'

'That 's what happened to the slugs.'

'Did you ever hear the old Welsh law,' asked the landlord, 'that if you were to kill a cat or a dog belonging to another, the owner could tie the animal up by the tail till only its nose was touching the ground, and then you 'd have to pour wheat over him until he be covered, and the wheat would go to the owner?'

'A tidy lot of wheat to cover that sheep-dog o' yours,' said Jack.

'I 'd come off better than you with that little terrier of yours.'

'I shouldn't 'a' trimmed his tail so short,' said Jack.

Jack had but recently had an accident with his gun. It had gone off when he was getting over a fence. Unfortunately when it did go off it was pointing at a pheasant, and, more unfortunate still, the accident took place just behind the gamekeeper's cottage, Jack being a newcomer to the district. It was a pity he couldn't find his licence, too; he must have lost it when travelling. He had just had a letter from the court saying there were several small accounts to be settled. 'It 's different down my way,' he said.

'There's a proper fine chairman o' magistrates there. He'd break the heart of any sergeant o' police.'

It was ten o'clock and time to go. The old man was walking back along the same road as myself. The landlord came with us for a mile to exercise his spaniel. With the long evenings it was still light.

'I dreamt I was in court myself last night,' said the old man as we went along. 'Well, 'twas a queer dream, for I thought to be going to the bank, but 'twas in a court I found myself. Round by the back door they told me I must go. So I went round by the back door, and then I had to go down a passage where there was scaffolding, as if they was building something. I had to get down on my two knees to go under that scaffolding. When I did pass through it, there was the manager's office in front of me, but, before I could go inside, they made me take off my boots. Too muddy they said they was. We didn't do nothing inside, but when I came out the leather of my boots was hard as iron. Whatever I did I could not make my feet go into them. It was trying to put my feet into them boots that woke me up.'

'How's things at home?' asked the landlord.

'Well, my son is wanting to buy a little business in the town.'

'Has he got the money?'

'We thought to borrow it.'

'Some people builds big houses on lending money,' said the landlord.

'That's true enough.'

'Some people loses small houses by borrowing money.'

'I'd say they might.'

'A man who mortgages his farm wears hard and tight shoes ever after.'

The old man thought awhile on this. 'Well, I'll be damned,' he said.

'And he's down on his knees and through the back door all the rest of his life,' added the landlord.

'Well, I'll be damned,' said the old man again. Then he turned up the lane towards his house.

CHAPTER THIRTY-TWO

To APPRECIATE TO THE FULL any aspect of the country-side we must have watched that particular landscape through all its phases of the year. The richness of the green thigh-deep bracken on a hillside in summer is felt more strongly by those who have trodden the tattered red fern in winter. The sprightliness of the crimson larch flowers in spring is more thrilling to those who have seen the same branches sprayed with snow. The swirl of the November flood is heard with greater intensity by those who have listened to the soft burblings of summer.

On warm evenings in spring I go out and sit on one of the ridges overlooking the dingle, through which trickles the over-flow from my lake. Steep time-worn slopes, a hundred feet and more from their summits to the water at their feet. In winter there was scarcely a stir of life; now, on all sides, there is a thrust and urge. Birds are flitting where dead leaves whirled. The wild rose, still stippled with last year's scarlet berries, is breaking into leaf. In December, stripes of bright green marked the un-frozen springs; now, all the hills shine emerald in the evening sun. In January, when the sky lowered darker than the fir-trees on the mountain, the shepherds were collecting their sheep before the coming snow; now, when the primroses and violets are scenting the air and the wood sorrel is dappling the shady nooks, they are rounding up the young lambs to count them and mark them with daubs of ownership.

For the most part the slopes are bracken-covered, with patches of gorse and bramble, but there are also rocks and stones laid bare by the winter's storms. On these, already, spores and small seeds have lodged, and soon, when lichens and algae are veiling their surface, fine roots will be eating into their substance, dis-integrating and preparing it for stronger-growing plants. Mosses will then take hold and ferns will drive deep into the crevices, and the decaying fibres of both will, in time, add humus to the accumu-lating soil. Then will come the bracken and the gorse, the ivy and the whortleberry, and they will remain the masters until fir-trees usurp their kingdom or landslides begin another cycle. So, in one series or another, these long-drawn successions occur until the climax is reached, and there is nothing strong enough, save man or some cataclysm of nature, to displace the last dominating arrival.

Man and his animals interfere with many of these successions in more ways than are at first obvious. Apart from the clearing and cultivation of land, and the grazing of his animals who nip off the tender tips of woody seedlings, there is, for example, his constant war on 'vermin.' This so upsets the balance of nature that mice and moles have increased prodigiously. These small rodents not only eat the nuts of the oak, beech, and hazel, and gnaw the bark of the seedlings, but they burrow underground and nibble the young roots. It has been said by one who has devoted his life to this subject that they are probably the chief agents in preventing the natural regeneration of our forests. Another authority has given, as his opinion, that if man and his animals were to disappear from Britain the greater part of the island would revert to forests within two hundred years.

One evening, from my perch, I heard a peewit call. Again and again it came from over the larch wood, but there was no sign of the bird. Then a hedge sparrow warbled, and though I scanned the scrub and trees with my glasses I could see no sign. The only bird in sight was a thrush on a topmost bough. 'Piddy-hoo, piddy-hoo, piddy-hoo; chinny-chop-chinny, chinny-chop-chinny,' it called, and then suddenly with almost a laugh in its voice, 'peerweet, peerweet; pee-yip, pee-yip, pee-yip.' Once again it broke into its own 'piddy-hoo, piddy-hoo,' and then from its throat came the modest burbling notes of the hedge sparrow.

This was a surprise to me at the time, though Eliot Howard tells us that 'even the jay, than which few birds have a more raucous voice . . . will occasionally imitate the most melodious strains of some other species,' that 'the red-backed shrike, whose sexual call is principally a few harsh notes rapidly repeated, bursts at times into perfect imitations of the song of the swallow, linnet, or chaffinch,' and that 'the marsh-warbler can utter the call of the green woodpecker, or sing as the nightingale does.' He goes on to say that among birds 'there is plenty of evidence to show that the power of imitation is almost unlimited,' and from this he concludes that the diversity in song is not to be attributed to some

* F

structural peculiarity but rather to 'some innate capacity to play one tune in preference to another.'

The sides of the dingle are honeycombed with vole runs, and in the larches a brown owl, thinking of field mice, sits motionless, waiting for the dusk. A wood-pigeon, alarmed at my approach, leaves the wood with noisy flight: in contrast, a curlew rises silently from its nest in the rough bog that tops the hill. The nest, a cup in a tuft of heather, is lined with dry grasses, but young green blades, encouraged by the warmth in the nest, are pushing through. The four eggs with points to the centre are set north, south, east, and west. In *British Birds*, July 1931, George Marples tells how, following a suggestion from Mr. Hughes of Aberdovey, he made a series of visits to nests of the ringed plover, during which he not only observed the orientation of the eggs, but altered their alignment, and then noted if the parent birds replaced them in their original positions. He found that 'while some birds, almost invariably, replaced the eggs towards the "cardinal points" of the compass, others seemed quite casual about the matter.' But the former were definitely in the majority. In eighty out of a hundred and twenty-one observations he found that the eggs had been restored to their north, south, east, west alignment, and, of the remaining forty-one, eleven were nearly, though not quite, returned to their original positions.

Each evening the curlews come to wash in the lake. Wading in until their breasts touch the water they ruffle out their feathers, and splash their tails and wing-tips up and down in the water, only interrupting the action to dip their heads below the surface and throw a shower over their backs. One would imagine that every feather must be sodden before the bird walks back to the shore and begins to preen. Ruffling its feathers then to dry them, as a moment before it had done so to moisten them, it shakes itself like a dog, and with its flapping wings sends out a spray of rain. The ritual of preening is an elaborate one. Every feather seems to be dealt with in turn. It begins with a general combing with the bill, the tip of the bill being sometimes dipped in the water. Later the bird depresses its tail, and raises the feathers that cover the preening gland just above it. Then by running the bill along the gland it obtains the secretion with which it dresses the feathers. The back of the head is dealt with by the claw, but should the bird be standing in the water at the time it will, after lifting its foot and before touching the feathers, dabble its toes a few times lest any mud should be adhering to them.

And all the time the bird is on the alert. Every movement is followed by a quick glance around and upward; indeed, we who, in normal times, have little physical danger to fear in our daily lives, can have no conception of the constant watchfulness which is a feature of all wild life. We have only to watch any bird or

animal through high-powered glasses to see the uneasiness that is in its soul.

Across the rough moor, where the curlews nest, there runs a fence of wire and stakes, with here and there a thorn or birch-tree. Hereabouts is the territory of a female cuckoo. Whether or not a male confines his attention to the same area I do not know, though sometimes I surprise a pair together, and then I see the two slate-grey backs glide down the dingle accompanied by one, two, or even three meadow pipits. In Wales they call the meadow pipit *gwas-y-gog*, meaning 'the cuckoo's servant,' and it might seem that the term sometimes covers a wider range of duties than is generally accepted. I watched this female cuckoo sitting on the dead stump of one of the birch-trees. Around her fluttered a pipit, not in alarm or anger, as one might expect, but, seemingly, in pleasurable excitement. There was not the slightest suggestion of animosity; on the contrary, the small bird hopped from twig to twig as if glad to be near the larger one. After a while it dropped to the ground, and then at intervals flew to and from the tree as if to entice the cuckoo from its perch. For the most part the cuckoo paid little attention, but sat there with its feathers fluffed out as if indifferent to the proceedings. Occasionally, however, it would glide to earth, returning immediately with a worm in its beak. Unfortunately, from where I sat, I could not see what actually happened on the ground, but from the almost momentary disappearance of the cuckoo, and the obvious delight of the pipit, I had little doubt that the small bird was finding the worms and offering them to the other.

Mr. Edgar Chance, who has made a very careful study of the cuckoo's habits in England, even to being able to predict in what nest, on what day, and at what hour of that day a cuckoo will lay, records that while he was watching the behaviour of a pair of pipits towards a cuckoo who was about to lay her egg in their nest, one of the pipits 'twice appeared with a green grub which it carried and held with apparent intent to give to the cuckoo.' This seems to lend colour to what I have suggested. It does not follow, of course, that all foster-parents behave in this way. Mr. Chance is of opinion that 'the actions and reactions of fosterers run through every phase from violent resentment to comparative complaisance.' He says: 'The very sight of a cuckoo appears to arouse pugnacious feelings in some individuals whilst others show less concern. Some pairs even appear to welcome the cuckoo's intentions, for they will fly up and virtually invite her as she sits in her observation tree and escort her as she glides to their nest.' In what might at first appear to be support of the latter suggestion Mr. T. R. Livesey, a very close observer of the cuckoo, has described how on one occasion he watched the behaviour of a pair of chats towards a female cuckoo and felt sure, at the time, that they evinced pleasure rather than fear or anger. It looked to him, he says, as if the two little birds were trying to induce the cuckoo to patronize their nest, and allow them the honour of bringing up her young. Later, however, he came to the conclusion that the supposed solicitude of the chats was merely intense anxiety as to what was going to happen.

With these second thoughts of Mr. Livesey Mr. Stuart Baker, author of *Cuckoo Problems*, recently published, is in close agreement. Mr. Baker has made a lifelong study of cuckoos and their ways, not only in this country, but in many places abroad, particularly the Khasia Hills of India. There can be no one else alive to-day with the same mass of material from which to form judgments. Referring to the behaviour of my pipit, described above, he writes: 'I have so often watched small birds fussing round a cuckoo perched on a tree above or near their nest, and have always thought that their manners displayed acute anxiety as to what the cuckoo was about to do. . . . It is very difficult for human beings to interpret the expressions and attitudes of birds. This is rendered the more difficult in that the latter are often used to express very different emotions on different occasions. Most of the pheasants, partridges, and quails express courtship and antagonism to another male in exactly the same manner. The bitterns express fear, anger, and love all in identically the same position. Painted snipe certainly show off, the female to the male, in the same fan or semi-fan attitude as she does when she threatens another female, or when she is startled by something she thinks may be dangerous. The attitudes adopted by most birds under the stress of *great* emotion seem to be the same whether such emotion is the result of any one of their three causes, fear, anger, or love.' It would seem then that the apparent solicitude on the part of small birds for their parasite may be due to complicated nervous reactions far removed from what at first sight might seem obvious to a casual observer. The episode presents but one of the many problems of cuckoo biology. Here are a few of the facts which Mr. Stuart Baker considers may now be regarded as proved:

'Cuckoos search for and decide on nests in which to lay their eggs some days or hours in advance of laying.

'When placing an egg in a nest cuckoos remove one or more eggs of the fosterer.

'Eggs are projected into nests in holes into which the cuckoo cannot enter.

'The normal number of eggs laid by a cuckoo may be anything from twelve to eighteen.

'The eggs of any individual cuckoo are all very closely alike.

'Individual cuckoos always keep to the same foster-parent.

'The eggs laid by cuckoos often show close resemblance to the eggs of the foster-parent.

'Some species of young cuckoos eject the other occupants of the nest as soon as they, the cuckoos, are hatched. Some do not.'

Here are a few of the theories that still remain to be proved or disproved:

That 'the female cuckoo is neither monogamous nor polyandrous, but promiscuous.'

That 'parasite cuckoos take no interest in their eggs after they have been laid.'

That 'cuckoos are normally parasitic on the bird in whose nest they have themselves been reared.'

Those bird lovers who would like to gain intimate knowledge of the habits of British cuckoos should read Mr. Chance's *The Truth about the Cuckoo*. Those who would like to know about the cuckoos of India, Burma, Malay, Japan, Australia, and many other countries in Europe and America, as well as those of Great Britain, should read Mr. Stuart Baker's *Cuckoo Problems*. Those who would glimpse infinity should read both.

CHAPTER THIRTY-THREE

'BILL,' I said, 'I want to buy a horse.'

'A horse?' said Bill, surprised.

'Yes,' I said, 'a horse; a nice quiet old horse that I can ride, one that will stand still if I want to watch a bird, one that will mind its steps if I want to look at the country.'

'And one that will find its way home if it's a bit foggy,' said Bill.

'Thanks,' I said, 'that's put delicately.'

'What you want,' said Bill, 'is a pony.'

'Not big enough,' I said, 'I'm too heavy.'

'We'll get a big pony,' said Bill.

'What's the difference between a big pony and a small horse?' I asked.

'Well,' he said, 'a horse is a horse and a pony is a pony.'

So then I knew!

'You should have been at Newtown on Tuesday,' said Bill. 'April horse fair. A hundred and ninety in the catalogue. Lovely animals some of 'em, and lovely prices too,' he added. 'Twenty-eight guineas my uncle thought he'd get for his little piebald pony, thirty-six she fetched. There was heavy horses there that brought a hundred quid. Sixty, sixty-five, I reckon before the war.'

'When's the next fair?' I asked him.

'What for, to buy a pony?'

'Isn't that the idea?'

'Don't you go buying a pony at the sales. I only meant you should 'a' been there to have a look.'

'Why not buy one there?'

'Well, you want to know something about it, don't you? You don't want to bring it home and find it isn't right, and have to take it back again?'

I agreed to this.

'You want to find out about 'em first,' said Bill. 'No good asking at the sale. Guaranteed in any gear, they'll tell you. Yes, but you got to get 'em into that gear first. What's the good of a pony to you if you can't catch her? I know'd a pony was quiet

as a lamb once you was on her back, but you 'd got to get on her
back first. You want something 'll save you walking, I reckon,
not something 'll keep you running.'

A week later he said to me: 'Tom Hughes has a pony would
suit you.'

'Quiet?' I asked.

'His daughter was riding her to-day.'

'Would she carry me on the hills?'

'All day.'

'When can I see her?'

'To-night, if you like.'

We went along to Tom Hughes and I bought the pony. A little
over thirteen hands she stood, thirteen one or thirteen two. Her
legs looked like knitting needles to me, but they said she 'd carry
me. Dan Mills lent me a saddle. Bill lent me a bridle. Cobbler
brought her up to me, as nice and quiet and active a little animal
as you could wish. She comes when she is called. She stands
still while I mount. Betty is her name.

CHAPTER THIRTY-FOUR

DICK HOWELL has been a friend of mine ever since I helped him to find water. His farm is high in the hills, behind Llangurig, and it was there that I met him one day when I was looking for curlews' nests. He was mending his boundary fence and I gave him a hand with tautening the wire. The gauge had been all wrong, he told me. 'Whoever put up the fence was no trades-man.' It might do against cattle, it was no good against sheep. For sheep the bottom wire should be not more than three or four inches from the ground, and the two strands next above shouldn't leave gaps of more than four inches. Then might come an interval of five inches, and then one of six and then one of seven. The top strand needn't be any closer than ten inches, though it should be barbed, to stop cattle or horses pressing on it. He hadn't been on the farm long, only since the twenty-fifth of March, and he liked it well enough. But with the lack of rain there was a shortage of water. His well had gone dry, and he had to fetch all he wanted from a pool a quarter of a mile from the house. That would be dry too if the weather didn't change before long. He thought of getting 'one of them men with a hazel stick,' but he didn't know of one within twenty miles.

'I think I know of one and he's nearer than that,' I said.

'You do?'

'I do.'

'And where would he be?'

'In the same field with yourself.'

He took off his old green cap and scratched his head. 'Ar'oo a diviner?' he asked, astonished.

'If there's water there I think I'll know. But I can't tell you how strong it is, or how deep it is. There are some who can, but I'm not one of them. I haven't done enough of it.'

'I've heard tell of a man who could find a corpse,' he said. 'Followed it down a river he did till it stuck in the roots of a tree. "It's there," he said to the police who was doin' the draggin'. "It's there surely," he said, "I can tell by the rod," he said. Well, they dragged and they dragged, but they found nothing.

"It's gone down to the sea," said the sergeant of police. "It has never gone over the weir," said the man with the rod. I don't know what was his name. My cousin was telling me. He was living up Leamington way. 'Tis only a few years back since he told me.'

'The hottest day of my life was one I spent with a man in the West Indies, trying to find pirates' gold,' I told him. 'He was trying, not me. I didn't know I had the power then, or I'd have been after it too.'

'Did he find any?' asked Howell.

'Divil a penny,' I said.

'I've heard tell of a man who found shillings on the road before him,' said Howell. 'Not far from here it was. Well, it was far, but not so far. No one else could see them, only him. No, no, he hadn't a rod. 'Twas with his two eyes he saw them. And as long as he give 'em to charity he found 'em; every time he passed, one of 'em in the same place. Would you believe it, when he got 'em mixed up with his own and spent one on 'isself he found no more. I suppose you'll be wanting a hazel twig,' he added, after a pause. 'There's a hedge below by the house.'

'There's a thorn bush here will do as well,' I said.

'A quickthorn wouldn't do?' he asked.

'Quickthorn or blackthorn will do,' I told him, 'or sally bush or alder, or mountain ash or birch; almost any tree will do.'

He took off his cap and scratched his head again, but said nothing.

'We needn't cut any of them,' I said, 'that bit of wire at your feet will do.'

'This bit?' he asked, incredulously, picking up about a yard and a half that he had cut from a strand, after making it fast to the corner post.

I took it from him, and bending it in two, I twisted the two lengths together. Then I folded it as I have shown in the engraving. 'Come on,' I said. 'Where do you want water?'

'As near as you can to the house,' he said.

We went down the hill and through the clump of fir-trees above his farm. There I could feel activity in the wire, but I did not begin serious operations till I was in the meadow next to his yard. There was water every hundred yards. 'The place is full of water,' I told him.

Once again he scratched his head.

'Try it yourself,' I said. 'You are the owner. It should surely act for you.'

He took the two ends of the wire in his hands and held them as I had done, with the loop at the head of the V towards his body and the wire horizontal. Then he walked back over the ground we had already traversed.

'It don't work for me,' he said, looking a bit crestfallen.

'Take your time,' I told him. 'Get the feel of the wire in your hands. Hold it with a little more stretch on the wire.'

Again he walked across the field, but again he failed to get any response.

'One more try,' I said, and this time I held his wrist as he went along.

'By damn it 's moving!' he said.

'It is,' I said. 'Go steady!'

Slowly the wire rose to the vertical and turned forwards. Then as we passed beyond the main influence of the water it came back again, first to the vertical, and later almost to where it had been when we started. I let go his wrist. Again he took off his cap, but this time it was to wipe big beads of perspiration from his forehead.

After a few minutes' rest he tried again, by himself. This time the rod acted for him.

'Now you 're a diviner yourself,' I told him.

He didn't say much. Instead, he went into the yard and fetched a pick and shovel from one of the outbuildings. His son came back with him, and the two of them began to dig. At a depth of four feet the ground was moist. When they got to five feet they were standing in slush.

'Another foot and we 'll get it,' said Howell.

'You 've got it already,' I told him. 'Look where it is seeping up. Why, it 's nearly bubbling there by your foot.'

One could see, in the muddy water that had collected, tiny currents of clearer water making their way in from the shaly soil. We watched it for close on half an hour, by the end of which time there were several inches of water in the hole. 'Come in for a cup of tea,' said Howell.

When we got back there was nearly a foot of water. 'It will be full in the morning,' I told him. I was right.

The next time I met Howell neither of us was looking for water. It was at the 'Glansevern Arms.' I was out on a jaunt with Betty the pony, and I thought it might be nice for her to have a rest. Howell was there when I went in. A few minutes later a short stout lorry driver and a long lean man in riding breeches and leggings came in. The breeches were new, and somewhat extravagant in cut, but the collar above them was frayed, and dirty. He carried the ash stick beloved of all horse dealers.

'A pretty little pony outside,' he said.

Howell agreed, nodding his head in my direction.

'Care to sell 'er?' he asked.

'No,' I said, 'I 've only just bought her.'

'Just what I want,' he said. 'Got th' exact match of 'er at 'ome.'

'What do you want two for?' I queried.

'Got two daughters,' he said. 'Younger one just back from school. "Dad," she says, "don't you come 'ome without a pony for me." 'Er sister 'as 'ad one this twelvemonth. Make a pretty pair the two of 'em. Same markings exactly: blaze on the fore-head and a couple of hind socks. What you give for 'er, if I may ask?' he said.

'Nineteen quid,' I said.

'I 'll give you twenty-five right now.'

'I didn't buy her to sell,' I told him.

'My little girl 'd love 'er,' he said. 'She 'd be a pet o' the family, same as the other. Would you believe it, the one at 'ome comes into the 'ouse of 'er own accord. A real pet she is. I can see this 'd be her match. Twenty-five quid, right now. There 's a profit of six quid. What! Nothin' doin'? Well, 'ere 's my address,' handing me a dirty crumpled card. 'You let me know

if you wants t' sell 'er. Just the match of my little mare at home,'
he said, as I got into the saddle. 'My daughter 'd pet her no end.'

A fortnight later I met Howell again. 'Do you know what
that fellow in the breeches said after you were round the corner
the other day?' he asked. 'He said: "I ain't got no daughters, but
I could sell that pony in Warwick for thirty-five quid to-morrow."'

CHAPTER THIRTY-FIVE

WE WHO FLATTER OURSELVES on how far we have travelled from 'a state of nature' are still mighty susceptible to the listings of the wind. We are braced when it blows from the north, enervated when it blows from the south, soothed by the breezes from the west, depressed by those from the east. Reason, will power, and the warmest clothing are powerless against an east wind. There is something inherently pernicious about it. Even poor Job who lived hundreds of miles to the east of us was afflicted by it. How far one has to travel towards the east to get beyond the source of the trouble I don't know—my migratory instincts have always been to the west; but there must come a point where the wind that blows from the east will be coming from our west. Why should a wind from one direction affect one's whole constitution, mental and physical, far more than one of greater intensity and lower temperature from another direction? Does it carry with it a dust finer even than the scent of flowers, a pulverescence which enters into our blood-stream and disturbs our liver, brain, and bones? We know now that radiation can appear either as waves or as particles.

I am not, of course, suggesting anything as drastic as Virgil describes in his third *Georgic*:

> 'The Mares to Cliffs of rugged Rocks repair,
> And with wide Nostrils snuff the western Air;
> When (wondrous to relate) the Parent Wind,
> Without the Stallion, propagates the Kind.'

It is a pity that the south wind in these islands is generally associated with rain, for there is a mellowness about it comparable to that of good wine, a bouquet born of the sun, that bouquet which only the grape can store for us.

To me that particular balminess is always associated with leisured hours on tropic seas, hours, and days, and even weeks when the sea seemed to be of solid blue, smooth as the glaze on porcelain, with only the bow wave of the ship and the breaking of the flying fish to disturb the calm, long hours when the air seemed filled with all the scents of all the flowers that grew upon the islands.

It is well known that scents can recall to our minds vivid pictures of places we have visited. Schopenhauer said: 'We might call smell the sense of memory in that it brings back to us more directly than any other the specific impression of an event or scene even from the most distant past.'

But it has been denied that a mental picture can call up the sensation of a scent. There I disagree. It may be true that looking through the glass of a florist's window we do not experience any suggestion of the scent of the flowers within, whereas the scent alone of those flowers would have quickly conjured up their image; nevertheless, speaking for myself, a photograph has often brought about the most realistic sensations of odours which at one time or another have affected me: Dieppe on first landing from England, Port Said at any time, the Sahara, copra sheds beside a Pacific lagoon. And it isn't only pictures which have this effect on me; an idea, at times, is sufficient. I remember, on one occasion, I was expecting a copy of the book, *Bring 'Em Back Alive*, from the library. It was an account of how wild animals are trapped for circuses and menageries. The book arrived by the morning post, in a cardboard carton, and the moment that I opened the parcel I got the smell of ammonia. The room was soon filled with that pungent odour of soiled sawdust that seems inseparable from the cages of captive animals. I put the book back in its box and began to work. It seemed to me that the last subscriber to borrow the volume must have been a member of the circus then performing in London, and that in some way the volume had got tainted. As the morning went on the smell grew stronger. It became so bad that I was unable to concentrate on my work, and I had to put aside my gravers. I was about to write to the library to complain that a book should be sent out in that

condition when a friend arrived. I apologized for the stench in
the studio when she came in, but she, very politely, said that there
was no smell noticeable. Later I referred to the subject again,
and she repeated her assurances.

'Well, go over to that shelf,' I told her, 'and put your nose to
that box, and see what happens.'

She did so and said that she could smell nothing.

'Open the box,' I told her.

She did so; still the same result.

'Smell the book,' I said. 'Take it out and open it. I can smell
it from here.'

She did as I had told her. 'There's no smell,' she said. 'Try
it yourself,' she added.

This time when I took the book there was no smell: nor from
that moment was there any trace of it in the room. The un-
pleasantness had been due entirely to suggestion.

Of course smell and taste are queer things. Whenever I see
blood, whether my own or somebody else's, I always get the
taste of it strongly in my mouth. That may be a common experience; I don't know. On the other hand, it is universal that
if through a heavy cold in the head our powers of smell become
inert, we find ourselves, when blindfolded, quite unable to differ-
entiate between the taste of an onion and that of an apple. Taste
can only distinguish the four qualities sweet, sour, salt, and bitter.
It is to our noses that we must look for flavour.

It would seem, too, that scent is something which is absorbed
into the tissues. We put our face down to a clump of primroses
and, drawing in a deep breath through our noses, we sense the
fragrance at every moment of the inhalation. It might then be
thought that our lungs being filled with this perfumed air we
should be equally charmed as the current passed outwards again
through the nose. But such is not the case. When we exhale we
get not even a faint reminder. The scent has disappeared. It
has, in fact, been absorbed.

In answer to this it might be suggested that the sensory papillae
of our noses are only sensitive to inflowing currents, but then we
know that only by exhalations are the flavours of the choicest
foods and wines appreciated; therefore that cannot be. Whatever
smells we smell we absorb into our being.

CHAPTER THIRTY-SIX

THE 'GEORGE BORROW' takes its name from the author of *Lavengro* and *The Romany Rye*, who stayed at the hotel for one night when travelling through 'Wild Wales.' Readers of the book which resulted from those travels may remember how in Chapter LXXII he speaks of the inn at Pont Erwyd and its consequential landlord. If that landlord was anything like his grandson, my neighbour, Clifford Holmes, I feel pretty sure that he was not consequential, and that any breach of good manners or any lack of geniality between him and his guest was on the part of George Borrow. Glancing at almost any page of *Wild Wales* it is easy to see how Borrow would irritate people who were not accustomed to being treated as inferiors. His idea of 'conversation' with the maid at the inn at Mallwyd is to throw questions at her in quick succession. Was she a native of the place? Were her parents alive? Where did her mother live? How did her mother support herself? Were her mother's lodgers quiet? What did her mother do when the lodgers were not quiet? Of what religion were the lodgers? Of what religion was the maid? Did she always belong to that religion? And so on. Another time he goes into a bar, hectors the old lady about the quality of her beer, and barks half a dozen questions at her in quick succession. 'Is this house your own?' 'Have you a husband?' 'Have you any children?' etc. No wonder the impression of him which still lingers in the neighbourhood is that he was 'nosey.' The Welsh are a proud people, and rightly resent inquisitiveness on the part of strangers. If they themselves seem a trifle inquisitive about visitors they have a perfect right to be. It is their country. If Borrow had been a little less careless of other people's feelings he would not have had to travel far in Wales before he realized that it was the custom, then as now, for men to meet in a bar to transact business. There over a glass of beer they make their bargains. To interrupt them with ill-timed curiosity deserves

nothing less than the rebuke he received at Pont Erwyd when he
was told that his place was in the parlour.

The inn at Pont Erwyd to-day is as charming as any on the
river. Strictly speaking it is not in the Wye valley, being·on the
other side of the watershed, but it overlooks the Rheidol, and
the Rheidol rises in the same hummock of Plynlimon as the Wye.
'A bit cock-eyed, but you ask for what you want,' I was told by
the lady who greeted me on arrival. There was no need to ask
for anything.

From the terrace in front of the house one looks into a deep
gorge of tumbling waters. On either side the dull gold of the
oak leaves intermingles with the cool green of the rowan and the
birch as they climb from water's edge to summit. Bright patches
of whortleberries cluster on mossy ledges, and ferns bracket
the rock faces. Jackdaws nest among gnarled roots on perilous
shelves.

Washing myself at my cottage has always been a problem, for
to stand stripped before a quart basin in a draught that blows out
the candle is poor luxury. After a Spartan winter I evolved a
system which carried me through the spring with reasonable
success. In this I divided the body into six sections, and washed
one section each day. Right leg, Monday. Left leg, Tuesday.
Right arm, Wednesday. Left arm, Thursday. Trunk, Friday.
Head and neck, Saturday. Sunday, being a feast day, I had
a quick general rinse before the fire. It may, therefore, not
be difficult to understand my emotions when, after riding
fourteen miles over the pass in driving rain, I found not only
a bathroom in the hotel, but one fitted with an electric water-
heater.

Most of my readers will know the comfort of soaking in a hot
bath after a drenching in cold rain. There is, therefore, no need
to describe my sensations as I lay at full length with the warm tide
rising higher and higher about me until chin-deep I turned off the
taps with my foot. As my limbs lost weight I thought how comfortable it must be to float on water as water birds do, and I
wondered by what mechanism the diving ducks and grebes increased their buoyancy at will. Those who have watched these
birds diving will have noticed how on coming to the surface they
do not emerge fully at first, but show only their head and neck

and upper part of the back above the water until they have made sure that no danger is at hand. Then, probably by some extra inflation of the air sacs in their body, they rise to their more normal position.

I thought, too, of the wild duck who had appeared on my lake that morning, followed by three youngsters. They kept close to the rushes, the mother swimming with her head held high, ever on the alert, the ducklings bunched together so that they appeared as one bird. There had been no sign of a duck on the water since a morning at the end of April, when a pair explored the pool, their yellow beaks glistening in the early morning sun, and the drake's green head bright against the reflection of a grey cloud.

From the ducks my mind floated to the black-headed gulls who in the past ten days of stormy weather had not only built their

nests among the rushes by the lake, but in several cases had completed their complement of eggs. Two, three, or four they lay, most often three, slightly smaller and less pointed than those of the curlew, varying considerably in appearance, but for the most part of a warm stone colour, blotched and spotted with a darker brown.

My first indication that there were eggs in the nests was when I disturbed a crow on the hillside, and found an empty shell where the bird had been standing. These crows are villains, and are constantly robbing the nests; they robbed my garden, too, picking out each seed potato and carrying it away in their beaks. Still, I expect they make good husbands.

From my window I could watch the gulls adding to their nests, for they continue building operations after the eggs have been laid. While one of the pair sits in the nest the other brings it materials. There are plenty of dead rushes lying about, so there is no great labour in this work. The bird that brings them drops them beside its mate, then slips into the water, and swims round and round the nest as if enjoying the sight of the ever-mounting edifice. Meanwhile the bird on the nest is putting the new fabric into place, scrabbling it under the eggs with its feet, or moulding it against the sides of the nest with its breast. There is something extraordinarily impressive about such a colony of nesting birds. Day and night for three weeks one or other of each pair is sitting there, seemingly comatose, yet alert to every danger. There may be gales that sweep across the lake and rock the nests on their foundation of rushes; there may be the full heat of the June sun blazing on their heads day after day. It makes no difference. There the birds sit until the eggs crack, and the speckled youngsters appear. Even then there are many days of brooding before 'the young wings tremble, the birds take flight.' That phrase is from a poem by Dafydd ap Gwilym, translated by David Bell.

Many people to-day consider Dafydd to have been the greatest poet Wales has yet produced, and some even say that he is 'the greatest poet who has ever written in any Celtic language.' George Borrow, with but a dictionary knowledge of the language, considered him to be 'the greatest poetical genius that has appeared in Europe since the revival of literature.' Those of us who have not the privilege of the Welsh language can only be grateful to such translators as H. Idris Bell and his son, David. By their permission and that of the Honourable Society of Cymmrodorion, who published their work, I am enabled to quote the following. From a poem, *May and January*:

> '. . . The bitter battle of frost is over,
> And close-wove veils each thicket cover,
> Green are the paths where April trod
> Now May is here, and the woods are loud;
> Every oak's high summit rings
> With the young bird's lusty carollings,
> And every copse is sweet with song,
> And cuckoo calls, and the days are long,

And a white haze, when the wind dies,
Over the heart of the valley lies,
And evening skies are blue and clear,
And the trees ashimmer with gossamer,
And birds busy the woodland through,
And the boughs put on their leaves anew . . .'

And of *The Ladies of Llanbadarn*:

'. . . Never was Sunday that passed by
But in Llanbadarn church was I,
My looks for the ladies, signalling love,
And the nape of my neck for God above . . .'

Tradition says that Dafydd was born at Bro Gynin, about eight miles to the west of Pont Erwyd, and that he was buried at Strata Florida Abbey, about nine miles to the south. Round about and between these two places he seems to have spent most of his life. I must, therefore, have been in country well known to him.

From musing on the poets it was not far to thoughts of the harp, and the hot tap now gently trickling again was a suitable accompaniment. (Don't forget I hadn't had a bath for three months.) The harp that once through Cambria's hills is now nearly as silent as that of Tara's halls; nevertheless, there are men still alive who in their youth were taken into the household of relatives or patrons to act as minstrels, much as David was taken into the house of Saul. They will tell you of the great days of minstrelsy, and of the honour accorded to the bards. It did not matter at what time of the day or night a bard arrived, there was always a welcome for him.

'Who 's that?' called an old gentleman from his window late one night after the household had gone to bed.

'It 's Ceiriog and some friends,' came the answer.

The reply was a password. Everybody in the house was aroused, fires were rekindled, and the best hospitality provided. The rest of the night was passed in music and song. Dawn was ushered in to the sound of the harp. A harp could never be distrained on for debt. It descended from father to youngest son.

My reveries were upset by the scream of an old lady who was half-way across the bathroom before she saw me. I 'd forgotten to lock the door. And then the gong rang for dinner.

CHAPTER THIRTY-SEVEN

THERE ARE TWO FAMOUS BRIDGES near Pont Erwyd, the Parson's Bridge and the Devil's Bridge. Of the two, that of the parson is the more awe-inspiring, though the devil's is better known. The former spans the Rheidol gorge, and is no more than a few half-rotten planks suspended by rusting cables. It would be frightening enough to cross it were it over a calm and pleasant stream, but looking down from its crazy timbers there is a spectacle of 'antres vast . . . rough quarries, rocks, and hills,' which is positively terrifying. The river swirls and surges from pool to pool, scattering its foam in fleeces, and from the whale-dark overhanging rocks the water drips and drips and drips. Trees overhead stretch out across the chasm, and high above them tower fierce escarpments. The deathly scent of hawthorn fills the valley. The bridge was built originally so that the local parson might visit his parishioners on both sides of the river, hence the name. He is probably still its chief patron.

The Devil's Bridge was built by the devil himself, so I am told, to help an old woman whose cow had got into difficulties in the ravine. Thinking to add another soul to his already extensive collection, he made the bargain that if he did the building he was to have the first living thing that crossed the finished structure. But, like many another old lady, she wasn't as simple as she looked, and when the bridge was finished she threw a crust of bread to the other side. Immediately her little dog ran across, and the devil was foiled of his purpose. It was bad luck on the dog, but as dogs are easy to train, and without much conscience when their comfort is concerned, it is probable that he entered willingly enough into the service of y Gwr Drwg, the Evil Man. Indeed, he may be one of those very spirits which in the shape of a fiery ball, a round bowl, a goose, a bull, or even a lovely young woman, are sometimes seen going the road at night. The episode occurred in the eleventh century, and in all fairness it must be said that the Devil's Bridge is infinitely more pleasing in design than the two later contrivances erected immediately above it, one in the eighteenth

century, and the other, as its ugliness suggests, in comparatively
recent times.

Quoting from the guide-book, the Devil's Bridge is 'situated
in one of the most remarkable localities in the world.' Visitors
are said to be 'lost in wonder at the amazingly beautiful panorama
there outspread before their eyes.' The beauty of the waterfalls
is 'impossible to describe.' Yes, but what a pity it is being
exploited to the tune of one shilling per head, through a turnstile.

Back at Pont Erwyd the sun was dropping low, and shadows
were creeping up the eastern hills. One by one the cottages were
absorbed into the shade and their windows ceased to shine.
Swifts were flying in circles round the hotel, squealing as they
flew. Some say that these birds spend one or two of the short
nights of summer soaring at immense altitudes, but although they
have been seen to rise to great heights just before dark, it has not
yet been proved that they stay there.

What were men saying in the bar? That smoke was still
coming from Mrs. Jones's chimney: that it's a shame for her to
be living alone: that she'd die if she was moved: that she can't
last much longer. A young man with a bandaged finger had
been bitten by a ferret. 'Rub your hands all over with soft soap
before you handle 'em, and a ferret 'll never bite you,' he was told.
'Is that my neighbour gone up the road? I wants a word with
him,' said a middle-aged farmer. 'His sheep is gettin' a bit too
sharp. Three nights this week they been through the fence,
pulls the briers out of the gap quick as I puts 'em in. Pulls 'em,
mind you, pulls 'em *their* side o' the fence. No shape in that.
That man thinks he rises early. He doesn't get up too early
for me.'

In the corner two men were discussing a cure for warts. The
best way to get rid of them was to find a fallen star. 'You see
them shooting down across the sky,' said one, 'and you 'll find
them in the fields or out on the mountains. They look like frog
spawn, a kind of grey jelly. If you can find one of those and rub
it on the warts they will go.' He had had them all over his hands,
and his mare had had them all over her muzzle, until he found one
of these stars. He had rubbed some of it on his hands, and he had
gone down to the stable and rubbed some on the mare's nose, and
pushed some of it up her nostrils, and next morning both he and

G

the mare were cured. 'They say 'twas with the water from a spring that he found where he saw a star fall that Griffiths, the conjuror of Llangurig, did many of his cures,' said his companion.

If the weather was cold and wet when I was going up the valley it was hot and dry when I was coming down. Betty was fresh, and we were making good speed. Wheatears were flitting from rock to rock, titlarks were springing into the air and dropping again to earth not far away. A buzzard was soaring in wide circles. A kestrel was hovering high, its feathers like jets of flame against the sun. There wasn't a cloud in the sky. The Tarenig was sparkling on my right. It would soon be joined by the Wye from under Wye bridge. Suddenly a pair of lady's long white drawers flapped on a clothes line beside the road. Betty was shocked. So would I have been if I had had time. Being slower of thought I didn't go with her when she sprang across the road. Instead I met the granite road on the point of my shoulder. At first I was dazed and unable to move, but when I did open my eyes it was to see an exquisitely beautiful girl in R.A.F. uniform bending over me. Concussion, I thought. Then my eyes closed again. Next time they opened it was to find a man offering me a bottle of whisky. Bad concussion, I thought. Then Jack Tannatt, who lives near by, came and took me to his house. 'I'll bring the pony down for you,' he said, as later in the day, after much kindness, he put me in the bus for Llangurig.

'You should see a doctor,' said an old man in the bus.

'You *must* see a doctor,' said Gordon Poole, the driver of the bus.

'Who will I see?' I asked.

'See O'Malley,' said the old man.

'Best in the world,' said Gordon Poole.

'Kindest in the world,' added a woman behind him.

'I'll take you to his door,' said Poole.

So instead of getting out at Llangurig I went on to Llanidloes. But Edgar Jones, who was in the bus, jumped out. 'I'll go and telephone for you, say you're coming,' he said. 'Don't wait for me,' he called to Poole. 'I'll get a lift in later.'

'And it's Cork you come from?' said Dr. O'Malley, as he got me out of my shirt.

'It is,' I said.

'I'm from Galway myself,' he said.

'National University, I suppose?'

'National University.'

'I went there myself,' I told him.

'What course were you taking?'

'Well, my people thought it was medicine, but I think myself it was snipe shooting.'

'Cork is a grand county for snipe,' said O'Malley.

'Have you ever been to the city?' I asked.

'I've played there in matches. 'Twas there they broke my nose at hurley,' he said as he ran his fingers over my ribs. 'They carried me to the side of the field and there they left me till the match was over. D'you know, myself and the two policemen on duty were the only three men outside the touch-line when the game was over, all the spectators had rushed the field to join in a free fight.'

'Why didn't the police join in?'

'Oh, it was what they called a friendly match, not one of the championship affairs.'

'Well, if you have any ill will against Cork try to forget it while you're on my ribs,' I told him. But there was no need to admonish him; he was as gentle as could be.

'You've bust a rib and sprung a shoulder,' he said, 'and I think 'tis better for you to go into hospital.'

So into hospital I went, at Llanidloes. I was sorry to leave there a fortnight later, but I was glad to be back by the lake.

While I was away the rushes had grown so high that a clear view of the gulls on their nests was no longer possible. This was disappointing, as I had hoped to see the birds dispose of their egg-shells after the chicks were hatched. Some birds will first remove and then eat the empty shells outside the nest, others will eat the shells inside the nest, others will merely trample the fragments into the fabric of the nest. Most of our smaller garden birds just carry the two halves of the shell to a distance from the nest and then drop them. We have all found thrushes' and blackbirds' eggs on our lawns at one time or another; perhaps too a blue tit's, a chiff-chaff's, or a tree creeper's. Snipe rarely, if ever, remove the shells, and most of the ducks, including the teal, are equally lazy. A bittern has been seen on more than one occasion to hold a half shell under water until it was full, thereby making sure that it would sink. The black-headed gull either ejects the larger pieces of shell over the side of the nest or carries them away, trampling the smaller ones into the nest.

Mr. F. B. Kirkman, writing of 'The Birth of a Black-headed Gull' in *British Birds*, vol. xxiv, No. 10, says: 'If towards the end of the third week of incubation the eggs in a black-headed gull's nest be examined, there will be found on the surface of one of them an area of light cracks. This area extends until it occupies about a quarter of the circumference of the shell at its bigger end. If the egg is put to the ear a rhythmic tapping is clearly audible. . . . One hears also a repeated cheeping, which makes it evident that the chick has already penetrated the inner shell membrane dividing it from the air chamber provided by Nature at the bigger end of the egg, and that it has begun direct breathing. After thirty or forty hours or so the persistent tapping on the inner surface results in a small, clean-cut hole being drilled somewhere in the cracked area. . . . Through this hole the tip of a moving beak is visible.' After discussing the enlargement of that hole he continues: 'It is well known that the instrument used for making a breach in the shell by all birds and also by reptiles, including the crocodile, is the so-called egg-tooth. In birds it is a small, chalky, peak-shaped projection on the tip of the upper mandible of the beak. It appears a few days before birth, and, having performed its unique function, disappears gradually after the chick's exit from the egg.' He then tells us that the tapping is automatic, due probably to the onset of lung breathing, and that the perforation of the egg is therefore an involuntary act. Not only that, but the movements by which the chick breaks from the egg are also involuntary and are often continued for nearly an hour after hatching.

Now, while I am writing, the water is dotted with these small mottled birds and the sky above is filled with clamorous parents.

The black-headed gull is a wide traveller. Birds ringed in England have been recovered in the Azores, Spain and Portugal, and West Africa. Birds ringed in Sweden have been found in Essex, Norfolk, and Middlesex. One from Finland was recovered in Scarborough, one from Bohemia was picked up near Bristol.

CHAPTER THIRTY-EIGHT

IF I HAD BEEN ASKED to choose which bird should nest beside my cottage I could not have hoped for any better than the redstart. Other birds may be as gay in colour, but few can be so full of charm, flitting here, flitting there, now through the thicket like a wren, now over the hedge like a robin; up into the larch-trees like a warbler, back to the eaves like a tit; all the time its firetail gleaming, from every perch its call: 'hweet! hweet!'

It was an evening in May after heavy rain when a pair of these birds arrived. The wind from the south was dropping and clouds in the upper air were crossing from the west. Squalls were still darkening the face of the water, but glints of blue sky showed momentarily behind the clouds. Then for a moment the red-and-yellow edge of a rainbow was visible in the east. When I looked again to the west there was the black throat and flame-coloured breast of a cock redstart perched on the extreme tip of a straggling spray of thorn not a dozen yards from my door. The hen, more modest, both in colouring and behaviour, was flitting from twig to twig closer to the ground.

Almost immediately the two birds began prospecting for a site for their nest, each in turn exploring the walls and eaves of the old barn, and the more battered trees beside it. While one bird was away the other remained in the thorn bush as if guarding it, its tail all the time quivering in characteristic fashion. They did not seem to reach any decision that evening, nor could I see any point of focus for their activities next day, but on the third afternoon the hen was carrying grass in her beak. In and about the thorns she flitted, then in and out of a laurel bush, then up into the larch-trees. I watched her from secluded corners for the greater part of the next day with no success. If I was in front of the cottage or the barn she seemed to be busy behind the building, if I was behind either of the buildings she was elsewhere. But all the time that thorn bush was their rendezvous, and always the cock liked the extreme tip of that straggling branch. Perched

183

there against a background of dark trees his white forehead shone like a silver coronet, his breast like a cuirass of gold. He seemed as a young prince, active, alert, gay, and gloriously apparelled. Compared with him a bullfinch would be a fat old emperor, too proud and lazy for exertion.

Those birds still eluded me when I set out for Pont Erwyd. When I got back from hospital nearly three weeks later the first thing that I noticed was the hen with an insect in her beak.

'Cobbler,' I said, 'I *must* find that nest.' Cobbler had come back with me 'to settle me in.' 'Right, sir!' said Cobbler. That's what he says to every suggestion of mine, whether it is that he should go up inside the chimney to remove a charring beam, or that a crate of books in the village could be carried over the hill on his back. At this particular moment he was fetching a store of firewood. 'She's gone round to the back,' he said. So he dumped the kindling, and we both crept behind the house. But there was no sign of her there. We searched the eaves and gutters, and every crevice in the stones. Then we saw her low down by the barn. That's where she is, we thought. But she wasn't. 'It must be in some hole in one of the trees,' I said. Just then the two birds were flitting together through the wood. The sound of the kettle boiling over distracted our attention.

As I put the tea pot on the table I looked out of the door to see Cobbler standing under the veranda with his neck twisted out and up like the stack pipe to a roof gutter. 'Don't move,' he muttered. 'I've found her.' Out of sight, under the eaves, but immediately over my bedroom window, she had built. When I went upstairs a golden feather had fluttered into the room, and when I listened I could hear the movements of the young birds.

Apart from the ever-quivering tail it is the contrast of black face and throat with the brilliant gold breast which makes this bird so lovely. Black is a wonderful foil to other colours. Think how skilfully the Dutch painters used it, and the French Impressionists. How Vermeer enjoyed painting those tiles, how Degas and Manet loved to introduce a black hat. Perhaps the most striking examples are to be found among the Japanese colourprints, many of which would be quite insipid without the dark accent of a girl's head-dress.

The sight of a cock redstart always reminds me of a procession I once saw in Martinique. It was the fête day of the cooks on the island, and they were marching from the cathedral where a special service had been held in honour of the patron saint of their calling. They were all negroes, and for the most part women whose black faces and throats contrasted strongly with the brilliant silk and cotton dresses which they were wearing. These dresses were of Victorian design, and when the trains were carried over the wearers' arm they disclosed not only a wealth of pleated petticoats, but black legs in black boots, which again emphasized the gay tints of the underwear. The dresses themselves were of the brightest colours imaginable — gold, magenta, puce, sky-blue, lemon, crimson. On their heads they wore tight-fitting toques of gold tinsel, and following the open necks of their dresses fichus of as light and bright a material as anything else that they were wearing. Seen in the tropical sunlight it was the most exciting display I have ever witnessed.

Those same coloured women of Martinique raised a row when some humanitarian 'whites' tried to prevent their being employed for coaling ships. They won their case, too. 'Why shouldn't they carry a hundredweight of coal on their heads up gang-planks if they wanted to do so? In three days they could earn enough money to go home to the hills and be idle for the rest of the week.' To-day you will still see them in hundreds, with a girdle tied tightly about their loins, going up one gangway and down another, an endless procession from quayside to ship's bunker and back again.

Martinique is remarkable for the number of 'sole survivors' of the 1911 eruption of Mont Pelée. In particular, at St. Pierre, where the disaster occurred, you will meet elderly men who tell you how they were buried for days under the hot ash. They do not add that the one 'sole survivor' of whom this is true was a somewhat notorious criminal who at the time of the calamity was confined in an ill-ventilated underground cell. St. Pierre is a sad town. The ruined buildings still remain half buried as they did at Messina till a few years ago, and the inhabitants are weighed down by the ever-present fear of another cataclysm. The mountain is still hot, and the stream that issues from it is hot too, too hot to bathe in in places, as I found when I tried. The fumes that

rise from it are sulphurous as the fumes of hell.   In the hotel
where I stayed the little negro waitress wanted me to take her
back to England.   She offered to be my slave, she offered to be
the slave of any one to whom I would give her, if I would just
take her from the island.   Unfortunately I could not quite see
her fitting in with my Berkshire *ménage*; so I was forced to decline
the offer.

CHAPTER THIRTY-NINE

THOSE WHO KNEW the artists' quarter in Paris about the years 1920 to 1930 will remember how, for no apparent reason, the artists as a body would cease to patronize a particular café, and migrate to another which might be no further away than the other side of the street, or even next door. Then, three months, six months, or a year later they would as suddenly move back to their former haunt, or go further on to yet another.

Sometimes there was a reason for the move. I remember one restaurant in Montparnasse that was famous for its fish. *Moules marinières*, *langouste* in various dishes, and other delicacies could be had there in perfection. It was a favourite resort of many artists for years. But one day the quality of the fare deteriorated, and soon it went from bad to worse. No one could tell why. Then it became known that another establishment, scarcely a hundred yards further along the boulevard, was as good as the other had once been. Everybody patronized it immediately. It wasn't long before the news leaked out that the wife of the proprietor of the first establishment had eloped with the proprietor of the second. It was she who was the epicure in fish.

But often there was no such valid reason. It might just be the whim of one or two leaders of whatever movement in painting was then fashionable. At one time when I was there the 'Rotonde' was in favour. Six months later you were more likely to meet your friends at the 'Dôme.' Another time it was the 'Select,' and then the 'Coupole,' all four within sight of each other.

Although there is not the same choice of houses in Llangurig 'the boys' there are temperamental too, and equally liable to the migratory urge. During the summer of 1942 unofficial parades of the Home Guard were held at the 'Blue Bell.'

Living in solitude and sanctity in the hills, I rarely dropped down to the village unless my throat was dry, or I wanted one of those meals such as only Mrs. Jones at the post office can serve. (That's a grand place to stay, if you are lucky enough to get in.) One evening in July I called at the 'Blue Bell.' The house was full.

Dai, who had been away on munition work, was back for the week-end.

'What 's the fishing like?' he inquired.

'The river has sharpened a little bit,' said Ivor Morgan. 'There 's been a few good trout landed.'

John Manley was there. Had I got a ferrule on the blackthorn stick he 'd given me? Not yet, I had to confess. Bill Rhoscogh was there, with his bride Flossie. Tom Thomas and his brother Dan were there, and Dick Brown.

'Where 's Bill?' I asked.

'Must be at the "Vulcan,"' he said.

Tom Owen came in, after trimming a hedge. How was the hedge he had laid for me?

'Sprouting well,' I told him.

'That is good, that is very good.'

Trevor Jones was there too. He was also back from munition work. Yes, they 'd had a few bombs, but they couldn't hear them through the noise of the machinery. Joe Manley was there, and Ren Davies and Cledwyn Rees and Oswald Jones and Evan Rowlands and Percy Jones. Dan Mills, better known as Dan Clanach, after the name of his farm, came in. Had I had a bit more padding put in his saddle? I had. That was good. It wouldn't pinch any more. The pony had been very quiet when he 'd ridden her to the mountain with his sheep. Cobbler came in late. He had borrowed the pony to take a telegram a few miles into the hills. She was tied to the churchyard railings waiting for me.

It only needed ten minutes to closing time. The house was packed. Men sat on the barrels and on the tables to give more room to those who were compelled to remain on their feet. The daughters of the proprietor performed feats of agility as they carried trays of overflowing glasses through the crowd. Suddenly there was a hush, and then the whole company broke into song. There had been no warning, no discussion. It just happened. At first it was *The Golden Harp*, and then it was *Myfanwy*. Two others followed, and then the proprietor came forward and said that it was 'time.' Without further ado every one filed out. A few turned up the road to the west, a few turned down the road to the east. The majority stayed to talk by the lych-gate of the church.   Betty was restive with waiting, so I bade them all good night, and turned up the steep hill towards home.   I had not gone very far when there came to me again the music of their voices.   This time it was *Land of My Fathers*, sung as a hymn before they parted.   When I turned in the saddle to listen I could see the Wye winding silver through the valley.   Then the voices died away.

I rode on up the hill and across the bare moor.   Late that night I looked out of my window.   It was dark, but my lake reflected the stars, an infinity of stars.